SUCCESSFUL INTERVIEW SKILLS

THE TIMES

SUCCESSFUL INTERVIEW SKILLS

HOW TO PRESENT YOURSELF WITH CONFIDENCE

3RD EDITION

Rebecca Corfield

KOGAN
PAGE

To TB

First published in 1992
Second edition 1999
Third edition 2002
Reprinted 2003 (twice)

Kogan Page Limited
120 Pentonville Road
London N1 9JN
www.kogan-page.co.uk

© Rebecca Corfield, 1992, 1999, 2002

The views expressed in this book are those of the author, and are not necessarily the same as those of Times Newspapers Ltd.

British Library Cataloguing in Publication Data

A CIP record for this book is available from the British Library.

ISBN 0 7494 3892 4

Typeset by Saxon Graphics Ltd, Derby
Printed and bound by Clays Ltd, St Ives plc

Contents

Introduction

The importance of interviews

Imagine you have just received an invitation to a job interview. How do you feel? Elated, inspired and raring to go? Or terrified, resigned to your fate and overcome with a sense of impending doom?

Interviews are a fact of modern life and interview skills will be used by us all many times throughout our lives. Most jobs are filled as a result of these one-to-one meetings between the employer and the best candidates, but interview skills are needed in a variety of situations. Turning natural worries and fears into determination and dynamism is the subject of this book. Whether applying for a job, a promotion, a training programme, a college course, or even a bank loan, we all need to know about the processes involved in the interview and how to impress other people at first meeting. With part time and temporary work increasing, we will all be attending interviews more frequently in the future.

The skills involved in creating a favourable impression on others and presenting ourselves to them at interview are the same skills that make us confident at meeting people in any situation – whether at work or socially. If you know how to generate a favourable impression, have an impact on others and present yourself as an interesting and valuable person, you will be a winner more widely than just at job interviews. Your social poise will be enhanced in a variety of situations.

Interviews are difficult at the best of times. Whether applying for a job or a course, appearing before just one person or a panel, you need to know how to present yourself confidently and enthusiastically. Interviews are often seen as the major hurdle between us and the job we want. But an interview, whether for a job vacancy or anything else, is a marvellous opportunity. Why? Because you are in control of most of the impressions that the interviewer will form of you.

You, for instance, will decide how to dress and act, and exactly what you want to convey about yourself. No one else can *make* you look or behave in a way that you do not want to. In the same way you cannot be made to say anything you do not agree with. You must admit that this is a comforting thought. Although it may be difficult to believe, the interview will mostly go the way that you want it to. Of course, you will not be in control of the selection of the interview panel or the other candidates, but there are many things you can do to improve your chances of appearing as the best person for the job.

Many people think that it is a pure fluke whether they are successful in interviews or not. To them the outcome seems to depend on whether the face fits, being in the right place at the right time or some other unidentifiable cause. But the outcome of the interview process is *not* determined by chance. We can exercise considerable control and influence over the way the interview is conducted and, more important, over the outcome.

How to get the most out of this book

This book can show you how to exercise more control over interviews. Whether you are applying for jobs or courses at the moment, learning about interview techniques for the first time, advising other people on the best way to approach interviews, or just want to refresh your techniques for the future, this book will be able to help. For no matter how many times any of us face the interviewer across the table, we can still learn how to refine and improve our performance and put ourselves across more positively.

Some of the advice given may seem to be common sense but, when running training courses in interviewing skills and personal presentation, I am often surprised that such basic points need re-stating, and that is why they are included here.

Of course, I do not claim that this book will make you successful at getting *any* job, and I assume that you will only be applying for those vacancies for which you can reasonably expect to be considered. However, if we study the candidates who are successful at interview, we will discover some common characteristics.

Chapter 1 describes the interview process, explaining what exactly happens in an interview. Looking specifically at job interviews, we consider what the employers are trying to achieve through this process. Chapter 2 moves on to look at the whole experience through the eyes of the employer. It covers the most common mistakes and the recipe for success in interviews. Chapter 3 offers suggestions about planning and preparation, thinking through how to put yourself across and how to anticipate all the important aspects of the interview in advance.

Chapter 4 describes how to present yourself to create the best impression. It covers what contributes to the perception others have of us including body language, personal image and controlling nerves. In Chapter 5 the nerve-racking task of giving a presentation as part of your interview is examined, outlining methods of generating extra impact on your audience.

Chapter 6 moves on to give thirty sample questions that you may meet at your interview. Answers are suggested

The interview process

What is an interview?

The dictionary defines an interview as a face-to-face meeting for the purposes of consultation. In other words, it is a discussion for one reason or another. Organisations, companies and institutions use this method of meeting and discussion to help them choose the best candidates to employ.

By far the biggest cost to an employer is the staff or work-force. Wages and salaries often make up 70 per cent or more of a business's total costs, and the cost of advertising for staff is high. Obviously decisions about who to employ have to be taken seriously.

It is therefore not surprising that employers spend a great deal of time and money trying to ensure that they pick the right person for each job. In this context, the right person means the individual who will contribute most to the good of the company or organisation and who will repay the time and money spent on him or her as an employee by staying with the company and performing well.

Types of interview

Interviews come in many shapes and sizes. Not all interviews are to do with applying for jobs. For example, you may be interviewed for a place at college or on a training course, for voluntary work or to join a club or society. And overcoming the interview hurdle doesn't always end with getting the vacancy or course of our choice. Many of us will frequently be interviewed once we are in a job or studying, by our supervisors, managers or tutors. These interviews may be in order to appraise our progress, help us plan our future development or to resolve work or study problems.

About interviews

The people who interview you for a job are likely to be complete strangers, unless you are applying for a vacancy in an organisation in which you already work. Most of us would prefer to face people we do not know at interview as this makes it easier to describe ourselves freely, putting the slant we want on our answers. Finding ex- or present employers on the interview panel can be disconcerting and can feel constraining when trying to describe our best behaviour when the panel may have experience of us at our worst!

Interviews normally take place sitting down and can range from an informal chat in easy chairs over a coffee table to a formal panel interview (ie with a panel or more than one person interviewing) across a leather-topped boardroom table. More junior jobs tend to be decided by a one-to-one interview, usually with the employer or direct supervisor for the post in question.

Panel interviews

Panel interviews, where more than one person conducts the interview, are for more senior roles or where responsibility for overseeing the vacancy is divided between different people. An example could be for the post of a customer care manager. The Director of the organisation may be present together with the Head of Customer Relations and the Personnel Officer. In larger organisations a member of the personnel staff will often be present to ensure consistent standards of interviewing are maintained for the recruitment of all staff.

Other assessment methods

Interviews for jobs with larger companies or for more senior roles are sometimes part of a much more complicated selection procedure that can involve exercises, discussions, group activities and tests. These activities are designed to assess how the personality and values of the candidate fit those of the organisation and to test their intellect and ability. Often the exercises used are based on potential workplace situations. These simulations are intended to be more objective than just using an interview as they allow candidates to show their behaviour in a live situation rather than just talking about examples from their past.

Sometimes these selection procedures take place at what is called an assessment centre, often based at the head office of the organisation concerned. Although this conjures up a picture of a specialised venue just for assessing candidates, this is rarely the case. It more normally refers to the range of assessment activities that have been decided upon for a particular selection and the venue is the one most convenient for the organisation. You will normally be given an outline of the kind of activities that you will face which can give you the chance to prepare as much as possible for them. However, often the exact detail of the particular exercises will remain a secret until the day you attend the centre.

Tests can range from written papers to assess your personality, aptitude or abilities, to informal social groupings to
assess your 'fit' into the group of staff with whom you would
be working. Case studies, role-play, negotiation exercises
and team challenges can all be used.

Tests will be used to check your technical or specialist
understanding of problems. Some aptitude tests look at
general abilities or your capacity to thrive in particular
employment positions. General management vacancies may
use this kind of psychometric test to see if you are suited to
high pressure group leadership. Some employers such as the
Armed Forces also put candidates through a series of
physical challenges such as an obstacle course. In-tray exercises for jobs that involve strategic decisions will ask candidates to work against the clock to analyse and prioritise a file
of paperwork, some of which conflicts.

You may also be asked to give a presentation on some
aspect of the position applied for, as part of the selection
process. If this is the case it will be made clear in your letter
of invitation to the interview. Chapter 3 covers in detail how
to handle giving such a presentation.

Why do interviews take place?

Interviews are held to gather information. In an interview for
a job the employer first selects those applicants who seem
worth interviewing. The next step is to find out which of the
shortlisted candidates (those chosen for interview) would be
the most suitable person for the job.

If I asked you to find out about somebody whom you had
never met before, you would probably choose to talk to that
person face to face. Interviews are just a common-sense way
for people to find out about each other and ask each other
questions. So, as well as the employer seeing you, you also

have the chance to make your own decisions about the employer, the job on offer and the type of organisation or company concerned.

If you are selected for an interview there is every chance that you will end up getting the job.

What happens in an interview?

After applying for a job, you will be informed that the employer wishes you to attend at a specific place and time and you will probably be one of a group of people who have been shortlisted or chosen, from all the others who also applied for the position, to be seen individually by the employer. The employer will have sifted through the applications for the post, selecting for the shortlist those who best fit the specification for the job and those who seem to represent having some kind of extra value to them.

When you arrive at the company, if you have not already completed an application form, you may be asked to complete a form giving your personal details. At the appointed time you will be called in to the interview room and invited to sit facing your interviewer, often across, or around a table or desk.

The employer will ask you questions for a period of between 20 minutes and an hour on average, depending on the type of job applied for and the level of your experience and qualifications. At the end of this time you may be able to ask the employer some questions relating to the position applied for. (Chapter 5 contains more information about the type of questions that you may want to ask at this point.) This normally marks the end of the interview.

It is quite common for the interviewer to take notes about your answers in order to remember the main points after your discussion. For some jobs you will be asked to prepare a presentation on your ideas for the position. If so, this usually takes place before your interview begins. It can be a valuable chance to put across ideas you think can contribute to the organisation.

What are interviews about?

Interviews are like examinations at the end of a course. You know that you have done well so far on the course, and you know in advance roughly what areas the questions are going to cover. In the same way you know that you have done well in the selection process up to this point, or the employer would not have invited you for the interview. You also know in advance roughly what will be covered in the questions to be asked because you have studied the details relating to the job, and you have read this book!

What leads to success in interviews?

In the same way as thorough preparation leads to success in examinations, so a system for approaching interviews can have the same outcome. Most of the talking done in the interview will be by you. This means that you can have a fair measure of control in deciding where the interview is going. Of course, you cannot set all the questions yourself, but you can calculate fairly accurately what subject areas will be covered and plan your answers accordingly.

Even the most successful careerist will fail many interviews, but still end up in rewarding and challenging work. The best approach is to try to present yourself in the best way and treat each new interview as a learning experience.

Points to remember

1. Keep an open mind about what you may find in the interview. More varied methods of selection are now being introduced.

2. Don't live in the past. Just because you were not successful in previous interviews does not mean that the next time will be the same.

3. Don't try and fake your answers in tests. Most are sophisticated enough to spot any inconsistencies in what you say.

4. Be yourself, if you are not successful it may be that a better job is just around the corner.

2

What employers are looking for

The only reason why you will be invited to an interview is because the employer wants to find out more about you to ascertain whether you are the best candidate for the job. Sometimes people believe that they are called in to be tested with trick questions or put under pressure. This is very rarely the case. No sensible employer can afford the time for, or the expense of, such games. You will be interviewed for one purpose only – to find out exactly who you are and how you would deal with certain situations likely to crop up in the job.

You are only there because your initial approach, whether through application form or curriculum vitae (CV), has interested the employer enough to want to know more. Whatever you have said so far has worked.

Case study

An employer called Stephens' Circuits needed a new supervisor for their main depot. They had an internal candidate who had been temporarily taking on the role for the last six months and they thought he would be ideal for the job.

However, they wanted to be fair in their recruitment practices so they placed an advert in the local press and Jobcentre. Four people were shortlisted from the twenty who applied. On the day of the interviews, one of the external candidates so far outshone the favoured internal candidate that she was unanimously chosen for the post. Her preparation for the interview, her knowledge of the work and her enthusiasm for the role won her the job. The internal candidate however, was embarrassed at having to sell himself in front of familiar colleagues and did not give any evidence that he would be the best candidate.

Even when your chances are limited in relation to other candidates, if you perform best on the day of the interview, you may win through to get the job, even when another candidate looks more promising on paper.

Providing proof that you are the right candidate

If you have been called for an interview, there is no reason why you should not get the job. To capitalise on your success so far, you must research thoroughly exactly what you put in your CV or application. Let us consider the interview for a moment. What is happening there? A strange relationship has been set up – we do not normally have to talk to total strangers about our background, experiences and personality in such a one-sided way.

The situation arises because the employer has something that we want – the job – and we are 'on show' to convince him or her that we are the most suitable candidate for that particular job. Now the most suitable candidate may not necessarily be the best in terms of either experience or skills, but will be the person who seems to fit in best and is most impressive at the interview.

Employers are interested in three main areas:

- your qualifications and skills;
- your experience and work background;
- your personality and what sort of person you are.

The most important of these is the last one. I have known candidates who fall short of the advertised skills and qualifications for a job, and often lack the requisite experience, but who still manage to convince the employer that they are the best candidates on offer. How? By stressing that they have the right personality to fit into the organisation and contribute fully to the fortunes of that company. Skills can be taught and experience gained on the job, if necessary – but you cannot change your personality so easily.

The most common mistakes

In my research with employers, these are the most common reasons for failure at interview.

- Not answering the question fully or properly, eg answers too short or just lots of waffle.
- Not showing any excitement or enthusiasm for the work.
- Not being clear about their skills and abilities, eg being too vague or too modest.
- Using pretentious language or jargon instead of normal speech.
- Not showing that they have fully considered all aspects of the vacancy, eg indicating a dislike of paperwork when it is obvious that it is a large part of the job on offer.
- Having a sloppy appearance or too relaxed an attitude to the vacancy.

What the employer is looking for

PERSONALITY

EXPERIENCE

SKILLS/ABILITY

Reasons for success

Qualities in demand by most employers include being flexible; having a caring and helpful attitude to clients, customers and colleagues; enjoying working in a team; looking smart; showing keenness to take on responsibility for organising people or projects; being positive in your attitude in the face of difficulties or changes and displaying enthusiasm for the work. Evidence of continual learning is impressive, as is evidence of being able to handle change.

De-mystifying the interview

Employers are often bad at interviewing people. Have you ever had an interview where the employer did all the talking, or where he or she just did not manage to put you at ease at all, or where he or she arrived late and seemed confused about the exact job applied for? This sort of thing can happen when the interviewer is either not competent, not trained or not prepared for the occasion. Many people who are roped in to conduct interviews have had little or no formal training in this subject. Even if they have, it takes the right kind of personality to be good at interviewing other people and bring out interviewees' good points. It may surprise you to know that most interviewers are fearful when conducting interviews and display high levels of anxiety about the task.

However, defects in an interviewer's technique need not matter too much, although it can be helpful to be forewarned about such a possibility. Ultimately, it is up to you to prepare yourself so well that the interviewer's shortcomings will not distract you from putting your skills, experience and personality over positively. **You need to convince the employer that you have a lot to offer the company.** Let us think about this from the employer's point of view.

Stressing your contribution

Imagine that you run a company and need to employ an administrator. You already know that *everyone* who applies wants the job, and that it would improve their career prospects should they be successful. You do not necessarily want to hear at the interview how beneficial it would be for the candidates to get the job, because all the applicants will feel the same way. So do not be tempted to explain how you are looking for exactly this kind of job as it fits neatly into your career plan.

As the employer you want to hear what the candidates are going to offer *you* and what they can contribute to your organisation. The days have long gone since employers had difficulty in attracting applicants for vacancies. Now, assuming that you have advertised appropriately, you will have a good selection of people applying for your vacancy. Hundreds of applications arrive for some vacancies. The main question that you want answered is: 'Which one of the people I am interviewing today would offer most as an employee?'

Points to remember:

1. If you have been called for an interview, there is no reason why you should not get the job.

2. The candidate who performs best on the day will usually get the job.

3. The most important factor to convey is that you are the right sort of person for the job.

4. Employers are often bad at interviewing people.

5. You need to convince the employer that you have a lot to offer.

The importance of planning and preparation

Dos and don'ts

Do   spend some time thinking about yourself, your background and your strengths.

Do   come up with examples and illustrations to justify the claims you make about yourself.

Do   put yourself in the employer's shoes when thinking about what will work in the interview.

Don't   leave researching the employer and the vacancy too late, it can take time.

Don't   tell too many people that you have got an interview in case you do not get the job.

Don't   get frightened. Allow your interest in the job to let your enthusiasm grow.

3

Making a presentation

Giving a presentation

Sometimes you will be asked to give a short presentation as part of the interview. This will not be sprung on you. The employer will have explained what is required when you were invited for the session. If the letter sent does not make it completely clear what you have to do, do not hesitate to ring up and ask for more information.

Presentations are normally only requested if public speaking is central to the position applied for, eg public relations assistant, training officer, marketing executive. Any managerial position involves talking to groups of staff and an employer may use a presentation exercise to assess your leadership qualities. They are a way of giving you a block of time in which to make your case in whichever way you like. This means that you have the chance to provide extra information about why you think you would be the best person for the job.

Importance of planning and preparation

Imagine that you have applied for a job you very much want. Today, 'plop' on to the doormat, comes a letter inviting you for an interview. Congratulations! So far everything you have done has impressed the employer. Now that we have more of an idea of the principles behind the interviewing process, we can look in more detail at what to say. PLANNING and PREPARATION give you CONFIDENCE which leads to ENTHUSIASM and SUCCESS.

Planning your presentation

First comes the planning stage. Let us examine the heart of the question – how can you know what you should say in the interview? As indicated earlier, the interview is like an examination where you have been told the main subject areas for questioning in advance. The source of your information comes from what you have already been told or have found out about the job on offer.

You are being asked to give a presentation to explore how clearly you can:

- arrange material in a concise manner;
- explain key points clearly;
- have an impact on an audience.

A good presentation needs planning and rehearsal time to be confidently executed. Do not make the mistake of thinking that you can speak without at least as much preparation as you are giving to your answers to the interview questions that may crop up.

Your task is made easier if you have been told the topic of the presentation in advance of the interview. You can then spend enough time thinking about the title you have been given in order to get ready for the day.

Sometimes, although you are alerted in your letter of invitation to the interview that you will be asked to make a presentation, you may not be informed of the topic in advance. If this is the case, you will normally be allocated preparation time on the day, often an hour, in order to collect your thoughts and ideas to present to the interview panel. Do not panic if you find yourself in this position. It is rare for the topic to be completely unexpected. It is likely to be concerned with some aspect of the job concerned, as in this way the panel can get you to present a large amount of the information they need to assess in a concise manner.

Types of presentation

Here are some examples of different presentation topics that could be set:

- Prepare a five-minute outline of your ideas for developing this position.

- Have ready a 15 minute presentation on one of your priorities in this role.

- We would like you to talk for ten minutes on the key issues you think are facing this organisation.

- Please have ready a ten-minute outline of your main work achievements to date.

- Tell us in five minutes or less why we should give you this job.

- Explain to us in 15 minutes how you see the main strengths, weaknesses, opportunities and threats facing this company.

Exercises can include simulations of aspects of the job you are applying for, (for example, an in-tray exercise for a senior administrative position). Here you could be asked to read various documents as if they were in an in-tray awaiting your views, decisions and actions. One letter may be about a problem between members of staff; another e-mail may cover the need for a group meeting on a strategic matter where you need to set the agenda and another document may be asking for your views on a technical problem. You would be judged on your ability to prioritise, make decisions and manage varied situations according to the way you dealt with and responded to the documents in this simulation. Knowing the organisation concerned and feeling clear about the priorities that exist there will help you tackle this kind of activity. For instance, in an in-tray exercise of the kind described above, which element would you give priority to?

Discussions are often used for jobs or courses involving a high level of people-skills. They may take place with other candidates, sometimes with other staff, sometimes both together. An example of this kind of approach is with some senior Civil Service appointments where candidates are asked to give advice on a topical subject to someone acting in the role of the Government Minister in whose department the job is located. You could be given topics to debate under observation and will often be assessed on your ability to work with the group rather than just how you convey your own opinions. This means that helping others to join in and encouraging full and open debate could be more important than winning the arguments. If you may face this kind of activity, you need to have thought through your tactics in advance. For instance, in a sales environment, your ability to 'tune in' to others, tailor your conversation to theirs and reach mutual agreement might be impressive, whereas for a political researcher's job, thorough and detailed analysis may point to success.

Case study

One national organisation makes all candidates for management positions give a presentation. However, this presentation is not in front of the interview panel. Instead it is given to the very team of staff that the candidate will be managing if they are successful. The subject of the presentation is *why I want this job and how I would do it*. The team of staff are afterwards asked for their perceptions of the strengths and weaknesses of each presentation. The subsequent panel interview makes the final choice of candidate but the team's feedback is always taken into account. The most successful candidates concentrate on describing their management style and approach to working with teams rather than trying to second-guess exactly what the wider team is currently working on.

Preparing a presentation

You need to prepare a presentation even more fully than just a straightforward interview. First spend time thinking about the question if you have been set it in advance: talk it through with others, write yourself notes and mull it all over in your mind. If you do not have the question, and it will be provided only on the day of the interview, you can still do some valuable preparation. What kind of question might they set for you? It could be one that is similar to the examples above. Are there any particular aspects of the job that they might want to hear about? Is the organisation going through any kind of change or challenge at the present time? What do you think are the most significant parts of the job and how would you handle them? You need to be ready to talk on any of these points on the day.

Once you have some initial ideas, try and structure your session into three key points so that it is easy to follow. Do not try to pack too much information in, as a few clear points are better than a lot of confused material.

Rehearsing your presentation

No actor goes on stage without proper rehearsals, the final one in full dress. You should do the same. Practise what you want to say out loud to get yourself used to the key points.

Practise in front of:

- a mirror, so that you know how you are going to look;
- friends, so that you can check that what you are saying makes sense;
- the clock, so that you can time your presentation accurately.

Projecting yourself

Delivering a presentation requires a bit more energy than the normal interview because you will be giving a performance. Always give your presentation standing up if you get the chance. It is easier for people to concentrate on what you are saying if they can see you clearly. You need to present your material in a slightly larger than life manner with broader gestures, more projection and variety in your voice and greater animation than you might normally use. If you think your nerves might stop you performing in this way, you need to think of it as a show that you are putting on for the audience. You will only be asked to make a presentation if the job concerned means you will often be in this position. Think about the way that you would give group presentations if you were doing the job and this may help you on the day – you can imagine yourself to be in post already.

Using visual aids

Often you will be offered an overhead projector, flip chart or other visual aids to use if they would be a normal part of the job. Do not try and use anything that you are not confident or comfortable with. When you are under stress, it is not the best time to experiment with unfamiliar bits of machinery or computer programmes. Long PowerPoint presentations will not create as much impact as a well-chosen image or simple overhead transparency. Let your message do the talking, not the equipment.

Points to remember

1. Good presentations do not happen by accident, they have to be worked on.

2. The impression you want the employer to have of you is that you are the candidate with the most to offer and full of good ideas.

3. Structuring your presentation clearly will help the audience understand it.

4. Try to include some visual element to get your points across.

5. The delivery of your presentation needs as much work as the content.

6. Practice makes perfect.

Dos and don'ts

Do   keep it simple and direct.

Do   summarise your presentation in a hand-out or aide-memoire for the panel to keep afterwards, (make sure your name is on it).

Do   enjoy the presentation when you give it, to show you like this element of the work.

Don't   pitch it too high, you may go over the heads of everyone present.

Don't   talk in a different language to normal, avoid jargon and initials.

Don't   try to pack too much information into a short presentation, less is more.

Planning and preparation

An essential part of your preparation for attending any interview is deciding in advance your view of yourself, how you see the employer and your ideas about what you will do in the job. This is particularly important if you are being asked to give a presentation as part of the interview. This part of the process of getting ready for an interview could be called research and development, research about the job and how you view it and development of your depiction of yourself and your strengths.

Your view of yourself

Spend some time thinking through your employment history, especially trying to understand how your background will look when it is being considered through the eyes of the employer. Re-assess the information you provided on the application form. Can you clearly delineate your transferable skills, those that will be useful in the job being advertised?

How you see the employer

With the wealth of information available in our knowledge economy, there is no excuse for not finding out a great deal about an employer before you attend the interview. A useful part of your preparation is to discover as much as you can in answer to the following questions:

- What goods or services does this employer deal with?

- What are their stated aims and values or mission statement, if they exist?

- If a private sector company, how are they performing and who are their main competitors?

- If a public sector body, how much of a priority are they given currently with funding bodies and political decision-makers?

- How would you describe what sort of an organisation this is?

- Could you identify the organisation's culture? What do they believe in and how do they run things? How would it feel to work there? There is a huge difference between a traditional, hierarchical institution and a young, dynamic enterprise. In which would you feel most at home?

Setting up a system

The first stage of planning is to collect all the information you can about the vacancy and the organisation. You will rarely be invited for interview without being given some clues as to the sort of candidate required. If the job was advertised and you have been sent a job description or, even better, a person specification, you have as good as been told all the answers.

A job description, as the name suggests, details the main duties of the job and a person specification explains what sort of person the employer is looking for. Both these documents are very useful. Make sure you pay careful attention to all the paperwork that you receive about the job. The employer will have gone to a lot of time and trouble to write down what the post involves. You will be expected to show evidence that you have a lot to offer for each and every part of it.

Selling yourself

In the past when applicants for positions were much fewer, carefully working through these documents to show that you had the necessary experience and character would have been enough to get you a job. Nowadays, with so much more competition, it is not just a question of paying attention to detail but of finding ways to 'sell yourself'. Such an expression seems to apply more to washing powder than to human beings, but it is a good term to use.

Consider an advertisement for Sudso washing powder on the television. We are not just shown a box of Sudso and told to buy it. We may be shown a washing line full of sparkling white clothes to demonstrate exactly what the product can do. We are told repeatedly that it washes whiter; gives our clothes a lovely, fresh smell; is substantially cheaper than its rivals; comes in a refillable pack; removes dirt and stains, etc.

Because of all the other advertisements for similar products, the message is hammered home. But when we watch an advert like this, it does not seem as though the message has been too strong; rather, we are left with the impression that it may be a product we ought to try. This is the effect we want to create with the interviewer by using the invited time available to promote our strengths and positive attributes.

Analysing the job

The job description

By looking closely at the details in the job description you can see what the employer expects the job-holder to do. The tasks are sometimes split up into those where some experience is essential and others where experience is preferred. Ideally, you need to go through the following steps:

- Work through the job description.

- Underline or mark the words which mention the main activities of the job (the verbs).

- Make rough notes to show how you have gained experience of all these activities – think of an example from your background or work experience for each one.

- Convert your rough notes into a written or typed form that gives answers to questions on each of the points that you have underlined.

- Revisit the information that you provided on your application form, adding more and different examples as appropriate.

The person specification

This document is often sent out for vacancies in large companies, local authorities or the Civil Service, all of which have large personnel departments. It contains useful information about the type of person the organisation is looking for. Your approach to this information should be the same as for the job description.

- Study it carefully to see what characteristics are either *essential* for the job or *preferred* and underline both.

- Work through each of these items in rough, noting down an example from your own background which shows how your personality fits closely with what is required. You must provide proof that you have all the characteristics marked as essential to be successful in the interview.

- Write your answers in proper sentences so that you can rehearse them for the actual interview.

- If you completed an application form for this job previously, retrace your steps to fully prepare your answers on how you meet the person specification.

How to find out more

You may want to contact the company either formally or informally to find out more about their operations. By a formal contact I mean telephoning and talking to the person in charge of personnel or the local manager. For example:

'I have been invited for an interview with your company/ organisation soon and I wondered if there was any more information available about your products/services.'

There may be a specific question that you want answered, such as:

'Are all your offices based around London?'

Some people are happier not revealing that they are coming for an interview and simply say that they are doing research and want some information. Public companies publish annual reports which contain useful background on the major projects undertaken recently.

Companies often advertise their products or services in magazines, local and national newspapers, and on the Internet. These advertisements can show you how the company presents itself, and tell you which are its main products.

If you are targeting a certain organisation, you can look it up on the Internet. Search engines are fast and powerful ways to look up specific information. One current example is www.google.co.uk You could use it to look up words that relate to particular types of work or, to pinpoint information about a specific employer. You can also locate the job vacancies pages on the Web sites of those companies or organisations that attract you. Most companies now have their own Web site with up-to-date details of current vacancies. Often you can apply for a job direct through the Web site too, downloading application forms and then returning them or your CV via e-mail.

If you have a particular kind of job in mind but are not sure which organisation you want to work for, concentrate on job vacancy sites. Recruitment consultants, national broadsheet newspapers and employment agencies now run Web sites purely consisting of vacancies. The jobs they contain change frequently so you need to keep abreast of what they are offering. They normally allow you to specify the kind of role you are looking for and you can then be contacted by the site when something suitable arises.

Thinking about the job

When you are satisfied that you have gathered as much material as possible in the time available, you need to start thinking hard about the likely subjects to be covered at interview. To start with, though, consider the following advertisement, seen in a local paper:

STOCK HANDLER

Busy high street store requires seasonal stock handlers to work in their warehouse, sorting and checking stock. Training given but experience useful.

Now what can we tell, from this short advertisement, about the person required? Even without a job description or a person specification, and without knowing the name of the company, we can use our common sense to deduce the following. The person will need to be fit and healthy in order to carry boxes of stock around. There is bound to be a certain amount of paperwork and administration, involving completing and checking stock record cards, so the right candidate will need to be literate and numerate. Computer experience, or at least a willingness to learn, is always going to be useful.

The store is likely to be a large one if it has its own warehouse, so the work will probably involve working with teams of people. Someone with a friendly and flexible approach is needed. Accuracy will be important and care will have to be taken with the stock because of the value of the goods handled. The candidate should be honest and able to be trusted with valuables.

All these duties and characteristics can be inferred from the brief details given in the advert. We could get much more of an idea of the person required if we had been given a job description and a person specification. But even without them, there is no excuse for not thinking through what the employer is looking for as part of your preparation.

If you are not prepared to do some planning before the event, and do not feel that you can get excited about the vacancy, it may mean that you are not serious about applying for the position. Generally, if a job is worth going for, it is worth spending time preparing for, and that involves sifting through all the information at your disposal for clues about the candidate most likely to be successful.

Areas of likely questioning

It was stated earlier that an employer will be interested in three main areas of questioning. You know without a doubt that you will be asked questions about: (a) your qualifications and skills; (b) your previous work experience; and (c) your character or personality. Let us look at each of these areas in turn.

(a) Your qualifications and skills

Before you are interviewed it is helpful to have prepared a good CV. This document is useful for interviews as well as job applications as it should contain a concise list of courses taken and jobs held. Before the interview you will need to make a thorough review of your background, especially if you have taken several different courses. Fluffing your answers when you are unsure of your ground is all too apparent to an interviewer and looks unprofessional.

You will then be completely familiar with what you have spent time studying, and where and when. You almost need to be able to recite your CV in your sleep! As a result, when you are asked questions about your educational background, the information you require will come easily and concisely.

When you are being interviewed and are asked about your past studies, the employer does not want to hear you recite a list of the courses you have attended. Think *why* the employer should be interested in such information. The reason is that he or she wants to know *what you learned* from your studies. In most cases, therefore, it is more important to get across the main subjects studied, what projects you specifically worked on, which exams you passed – if any – and which parts of the course you enjoyed most, or learned most from.

Those who have not taken any exams will still be expected to talk about courses studied at school or college. You will need to work out which were your favourite subjects, which lessons you felt benefited you most, and why.

(b) Your previous work experience

The same is true of your work experience. All your jobs and the details of what you did as your main duties need to be at the front of your mind. You should not assume that it is obvious to an interviewer what you did as a filing clerk. Most interviewers will be interested in the precise skills used in the job that could help you to contribute to the position applied for.

You may think that all filing clerks file – but what sort of documents were you dealing with? Were they important legal papers or plans, originals of letters or clients' personal details? Perhaps you used to file things by number rather than alphabetically, or you might have had to cross-reference materials. Did you ever have to retrieve records in a hurry, work under pressure or trace missing papers? Did you ever use particular computer packages, answer queries from the public or liaise with colleagues from other departments?

All these things could be what are called *transferable skills,* ie skills that you learn or use in one job which can be transferred to the next. The advantage to an employer should be obvious. Your skill in one area of work, in which you can demonstrate expertise, means that you will not need training to do the same thing in the next job.

Again, let us consider *why* the interviewer is asking this type of question. The answer is, to see what kind of an employee you would make. Therefore, *when* you worked in a particular place is not as important as *what you contributed there,* since it gives the employer an idea of your capabilities.

(c) Your character or personality

Of the three main areas of interest to an employer, the greatest importance attaches to the type of person you are. It happens again and again; even if a candidate's educational background or previous experience is not up to those of his or her competitors, by demonstrating certain advantages involving personality or character, the candidate is successful in getting the job. Why should this be so? As long as a candidate is the sort of person who will fit into the company and who enjoys his or her work, that person can easily be trained to compensate for any lack of skills or experience.

Sharing the vision

There is one further aspect for employers to consider when they are interviewing. Many candidates may seem to have appropriate qualifications, experience and personality to fit the vacancy. What else could make the difference between the best and the rest? If candidates can show that they have thought about the job, specifically the contribution that they can make and the way that the job should be done, they cannot fail to impress.

This requires spending some time thinking about the key aspects of the job. What are the strengths and weaknesses of the organisation as far as you can tell? What can you discover about the environment in which the company is operating? Think about both the job and the organisation and try to analyse which factors might be important.

For instance, if the vacancy is with a commercial company, who are its competitors? What is your image of the product or service provided? Are there any changes taking place in the wider world that might affect the company's business? What about the nature of the specific job concerned? What do you see as the most important features of the job and why? How do you imagine yourself doing the job and what special contribution would you make?

Spending time developing your ideas or vision about the future for the organisation shows both your commitment and interest in the job and the likely added value that you could bring compared to other candidates. Most employers do not have the time to think about the specific details of every job in their organisation. They want to recruit people who can do the job well on their behalf and bring in fresh ideas and energy to the task. You will enhance the impression you make if you can also talk intelligently about your vision of the organisation and your role in it.

Mind the gap! Covering up your weak spots

We all have something we would prefer the interviewer didn't linger over. For some it may be time spent unemployed; for others it may be something in their past that they would prefer to cover up, such as a lot of job changes or having stayed too long in a dead-end job. Few people have a perfect career history, owing to various circumstances, eg having a family, a period of ill-health, previous or current unemployment, imprisonment or detention.

What is important is that you think through and practise how to deal with these gaps. It means learning, not how to lie, but how to put forward positively a cogent and convincing explanation of the relevant experience you have gained in the past.

Maximising your strengths

Another approach is not to cover up past experiences but to present them in a different way. This requires you to make a virtue out of things that happened to you through necessity. Let us look at an example. Imagine someone who has had several different jobs in a short space of time. The best way to justify this is to work out how this will concern an employer. So let us climb inside the mind of an employer who is faced with an interviewee called Deborah.

Deborah has had six jobs in the last five years and is applying to join W Sayer's company as a personal assistant. Mr Sayer, the managing director, is concerned that Deborah may want to leave this job in a few months' time. If that happened he would have to repeat the expensive and time-consuming task of selecting another employee. He is worried too that she will not settle into the position, that she will not take the work seriously and that she will not show enough commitment to the company.

Deborah realises that these job changes are something she should present positively to the interviewer. She does not imply that she was unhappy in any of her previous jobs but suggests that, even if she did not stay long in any one position, the employers were glad to have her even for a limited time because of the contribution she was able to make.

She spends time before the interview thinking about what she contributed in each of her previous jobs and what it was that made her want to move each time. In other words, she worked out her story in advance and planned what information she wanted to convey in the interview.

Golden rules

1. Always be positive about previous jobs

It is important always to be positive about *every* job that you have had in the past. Why should this be so vital? Again, let us consider it from the employer's point of view. Will it impress an interviewer to hear a candidate saying what a bad boss his or her last employer was? Will it sound good to hear another company being put down or maligned by a candidate, or will it make the employer think that the candidate could well be saying the same sort of thing about this company in a few years' time?

Someone who moans about other organisations also creates an impression of surliness and a negative attitude.

Nobody will be interested in employing such a candidate. The positive and keen candidate will be preferred.

2. Be enthusiastic and keen

Nothing attracts people like enthusiasm. The candidate who exhibits such a characteristic has a great advantage, almost before anything else is said or taken into consideration. We are all more interested in working with the person who comes into work each day in a good mood and feeling positive about the job, rather than with the moaner or troublemaker who is always being negative.

3. Capitalise on your strengths

The only things that the interviewer knows about you are what you have put in your application or CV and what you are going to talk about in the actual interview. Therefore, what you say about yourself dictates the impression that the interviewer will have of you, ie your skills, experience and personality. The interviewer will be looking at you as a potential worker or member of staff – you need to imply that everything you have been doing so far has been leading up to this job, with this organisation, at this time. Couple that with your vision of the way the job should be handled from now on. Irresistible!

Which questions to ask?

At the end of the interview, you will usually be asked if you have any questions to put. Do not feel obliged to ask something just for the sake of it. Only ask a question if it is necessary. If you feel that you know all you need to about the job on offer, it is fine to say something like:

'I think that you have covered all the important points already, thank you. But if I have any questions later I will contact you.'

Do not ask questions about uniforms, holidays or other practical points. If you are offered the post you will be informed about this kind of detail when you start.

If pay has not been mentioned so far, this is not the time to raise the issue. You would probably not accept any position without knowing the wages, but again you can find this out once you receive the offer of the job, when you could reply:

'I am interested in the job at this stage, but I am still not quite sure about the conditions of employment. Can you tell me exactly what the wages and hours are?'

If you do decide to ask the interviewer some questions, it is a good idea to show your general attitude in the type of thing you say. Questions about training opportunities or the chance to take on greater responsibilities in the future show that you are keen, plan to stay in the job, and are interested in moving up the organisation.

Points to remember

1. Studying the paperwork available about the job pays dividends.

2. Think yourself into the job, so that you talk as if you are doing it already.

3. Concentrate on what makes you more employable than the other candidates.

4. Try and make links between your past experience and what is needed in this role.

Creating the best impression

The importance of presentation

You may be asking why a chapter in a book on interviewing skills should be about presenting yourself. Surely the most important thing to learn is what to say in the interview? On the contrary, the impression we make on other people consists of much more than just the words we speak. A large part of the way we judge other people comes from first impressions. In other words, what we notice in the first quick glance, which may last for only 30 seconds, is the way they look and behave.

In fact, research has shown that 55 per cent of this first impression is based on appearance and behaviour, which can include clothing, posture, body language and facial expressions. Thirty-eight per cent of the impression is from the way we speak, which includes the way the voice is used, clarity of speech and accent. Only seven per cent is from the words we say.

Just consider this startling information for a moment. It means that a whole 93 per cent of that all-important first impression we make on other people is rooted in *what we look like and the way we sound*. We live in an increasingly televisual age where our information on what is happening in the world tends to come from a talking head and shoulders on the TV set. As a result we have become increasingly sophisticated in the level of presentation we expect and the degree to which we home in on distractions and inconsistencies. So whenever you are preparing for an interview it is necessary to spend a significant amount of time evaluating and considering the best way to present yourself physically to the employer. However, this is not information to be depressed about; on the contrary, it gives us much more control over the extent to which we can impress other people, especially interviewers.

Creating a positive first impression

If you are now saying that you personally do not judge others by such superficial measures, consider these percentages when you next meet people for the first time. Imagine you are at a party and want to make some new friends. Looking round the room, you notice someone whom you have not met before. She looks a bit dowdy and is standing alone with a worried expression on her face. She is looking at the floor with her shoulders slightly hunched and her arms folded tightly across her front. Although someone is trying to talk to her, she does not seem to be contributing much to the conversation.

Now you notice somebody else. She is smartly dressed, has a twinkle in her eye and is chatting animatedly to someone. She has just grinned at you in a friendly way, and you notice that she is standing up tall and looking confident. Which one of these two people would you be most likely to talk to?

The impression we gain about the first woman in this example is that she looks as though she does not care about herself much. She is not dressed up for a party and she appears uncomfortable and ill at ease as if she lacks self-confidence. The fact that she is not engaging in conversation may mean that she is avoiding contact with new people or just that she does not have much to talk about.

Now, of course, this opinion may be completely wrong. For all we know she may be a Hollywood star just back from a major film shoot, who is dressing down for the evening as a reaction to spending the last two months in film costume and theatrical make-up. She may be quiet and withdrawn because she only wants to meet new and genuine friends, not hangers-on. However, we are distracted by the contrast between her and the second woman in our example.

The second woman seems to be inviting attention and contact. She is outward-focussed, noticing the people around her and encouraging you by smiling in your direction. She appears to be a worthwhile person to try chatting to.

If we act on our positive first impressions of this person, our subsequent conversation at the party may reveal that she is a rather forlorn, needy egomaniac, but we would not assume this from her initial appearance.

In other words, we are highly affected by our visual impressions of others, particularly where rapid decisions have to be made (and an hour-long job interview is not a long time to decide on the best candidate). We will make judgements about the merits and demerits of people by picking up any visual clues we can – especially if certain individuals in a group stand out.

Even though we may not like the fact that we are being judged by others on their first impression of us, we are doing exactly the same to other people all the time. We all have prejudices about what we like to look at and what sort of behaviour we think is appropriate at different times. The secret of success is in understanding how other people perceive you and using this information to your advantage. Interviewers will make many allowances for a well-presented candidate.

The information in this chapter will be useful in many situations – not just at interviews. Once you know how to create a good first impression, you can be that person at the party whom everyone wants to meet! But creating a good first impression at an interview is doubly important because so much is at stake when you meet potential employers.

It is your responsibility to make sure that the impression you create works in your favour. This does not mean trying to put on an act or pretending to be someone else, as this will be obvious to the interviewer; rather, you want to enhance your strong points and minimise your weaker ones.

It was stated that 55 per cent of first impressions are created by the way we look and behave, 38 per cent by the way we sound and only 7 per cent by what we say. Let us look at each of these areas in turn. We will start by considering the factors that comprise the first two of these: appearance and voice. What you say in the interview is analysed in Chapter 6.

Appearance

I make no apology for concentrating on your physical appearance as part of your interview preparation. It can have a highly significant effect on your chances of getting a job. My aim is to get you to spend at least as much time on this aspect of your performance as you do rehearsing your interview answers. In the same way as the costume and stage make-up are pivotal to the impression of the actor on the stage, you are also going to be performing. You will have a short space of time, in competition with others, to make your mark. It makes sense to use everything at your disposal. Many more jobs have been lost by conveying a too casual attitude to the vacancy through appearance and body language than through providing one less-good answer. Our aim here is not to win any beauty contest but to ensure that our appearance is just right, provides no distractions and allows the interviewer to concentrate on our skills, aptitude and personality in relation to the job.

Your appearance is the most important aspect of the first impression you create. This cannot be stressed too much, and if it is the only thing you learn from reading this book, it will be valuable. The advice in this section applies equally to men and women. A smart appearance shows that you have taken trouble over the way you want to come across. A plain neutral look indicates a serious, professional outlook. Your choice of clothes indicates your attitude to yourself and other people.

It is worth spending some time thinking about the kind of appearance that is expected in the kind of job you are applying for. In creative industries the look is generally much more individualistic and casual. In more traditional sectors such as banking or the legal profession, the work clothing is also more traditional and suits are more prevalent, even for women staff, with more of a uniform appearance for all.

In the middle range comes employment such as teaching, local authority work and personal services that tend to exhibit more formality of appearance at the senior levels and a more casual look for junior staff. Once you have decided what the normal dress 'code' is for the kind of work you are applying for, you can choose your interview clothes by pitching your look one step up from the norm. For instance, you may decide to attend a job interview for a lecturing position in a suit whereas you would only wear a matching jacket and trousers or skirt for a clerical position in a museum.

Women will be more familiar with the points made here because they tend to be exposed to more advice and information about appearance than men, but this generally leads merely to lack of confidence. Being bombarded with messages about fashion and advertisements from the clothing and cosmetics industries only serves to worry women. It is similar to being spoilt for choice in a larger supermarket compared to the relatively simple choices of a corner shop – the shopping experience in the supermarket can lead to confusion. Interviews are difficult enough without adding the burden of concern about our appearance. The aim here is to eradicate this particular anxiety.

You do not want to appear showy or quirky in your choice of clothes but you should look clean and smart. I am often asked whether it is possible to be overdressed for an interview. I do not think so (with the possible exception of a dinner jacket or ball gown!). Even if the job would normally require you to wear overalls or a uniform, dressing with care for your interview shows you have taken time over your appearance and indicates an awareness of being, to some extent, on show. For instance a candidate for a motor mechanic traineeship may well want to wear a suit or jacket, tie and shirt to the interview at least, even if overalls would be worn once doing the job.

Men should wear a dark suit, or at least a smart jacket and tie for a job where less formal clothing is the norm. Women should dress smartly (a jacket is a good idea), and not be cluttered with accessories. Whatever the job, it is helpful when you are feeling nervous to add authority to the impression you create.

Colour and style of clothes

It is generally acknowledged that there is a particular range of colours that suits an individual best. These colours will be different for everybody but can help to give each of us a distinct presence. The right clothes do not draw attention to themselves; rather, they show off the person inside them, and in the right colours you will receive compliments on how well you are looking rather than on your clothes. Looking your best does not involve spending a lot of money on clothes, wearing the latest fashions or trying to look like someone else. A classic single-breasted jacket that you look after, will not date. If you have no money, see if you can borrow clothes from a friend or relative but do not squeeze yourself into something too small. Wearing clothes that are too tight merely makes you look bigger, use a size larger than normal to make you look smaller. Add height with accessories that accentuate the upper half of your body, such as a brooch or noticeable earrings.

As a rule, plain neutral colours are safest when you want to look smart. Navy blue or medium to dark grey for suits or jackets and a soft (not bright) white or ivory shirt or blouse work well for a confident, competent appearance. Black looks best on those with strong natural colouring or dark hair.

Don't confuse looking attractive or pretty with looking business-like. If you have long flowing hair, consider tying it back neatly for the interview to look more disciplined and practical. Keep your clothes that get attention for your social life and let your abilities and ideas do the talking in the interview.

Image consultants give professional advice on the colour and style of clothes to suit your natural colouring and body shape. The advice given is based on the idea of tailoring the colours you wear to those in the natural colouring of your hair, eyes and skin. The same applies to the style of your clothes. You have a certain body shape which can be echoed in your clothes to show you to your best advantage. This applies to a greater extent to women because of the more extensive range of styles and colours available to them, but it is also relevant to men – in particular to the shape and style of their clothes.

An initial consultation with an image consultant does not cost the earth. The money spent on one session of colour and style analysis with a good image consultant is easily compensated for by the time and money you will save when you no longer make 'shopping mistakes'. If you go regularly to a professional for advice on your health, hair, teeth, psychological problems, pets, etc why not go to a professional for advice on the most important part of your image? You will be advised which clothes make you look your best, what you will be most comfortable in, and what is most appropriate for different occasions. Look in the telephone directory for consultants in your area. Make sure you ask for specific advice about what to wear at interviews at your consultation.

Be aware of your appearance from every angle. I once knew a candidate who forgot to do this and only realised after the interview that her bright scarlet petticoat was visible under her smart black interview skirt. As the job she was trying to get was in a very sombre and traditional sector, she felt this may not have helped her chances overall.

Accessories

Ties, shoes, belts, bags and jewellery can make or break an outfit, although we tend to think of them as additions to our general look. Shoes are often noticed and should be appropriate, clean and smart for an interview. An employer I know says he looks first at a candidate's footwear. 'You can tell a lot about a person from their choice and care of shoes,' he says. 'The shoes don't have to be new but I'm always impressed if they are smart, well-looked after and clean. I would advise people to invest in a good pair of leather shoes because good quality shows.' This employer's field is public relations and he judges candidates' ability to present themselves as a good pointer to the way they would behave in the job. Dangling earrings should be left for evening wear, as should jingly bracelets. Jewellery is not generally considered acceptable on men and so remove it for the duration of the interview. Men should wear calf-length socks that stay up, in the same colour as their shoes. Women should carry only one bag. If you take a briefcase, put your handbag items in it. Don't juggle with both a briefcase and a handbag as it detracts from a well-organised, authoritative image.

Hair

Your hair should be clean and recently cut. If you have an important interview approaching, visit a good hairdresser and ask for advice on the best style for you. If you do this about a week before the interview, you will have time to get used to your new haircut. Most people look best in their natural hair colour, and this is evident when they are wearing clothes to complement their natural colouring.

Make-up

If you wear make-up, make sure that the style and colour do not date you. This is another area where women often lack confidence, because they are bombarded with conflicting advice from advertisements and magazine articles, but do not seek specialist help. Again, one trip to an image consultant can solve these problems and you will be given advice on the best colours and style of make-up to suit you.

If the interview is important to you, it is worth taking the time and trouble to wash your hair and have a bath or shower beforehand. Make sure that your hands are clean and your nails manicured. There is also no point in wearing smart clothes if they are not clean. Shirts or blouses that have not been ironed are particularly noticeable and create a sloppy look, regardless of how attractive they are. Body odour or greasy hair are not ways to impress any employer. Ask a trusted friend or relative to assess you for cleanliness and smartness. If in any doubt use a deodorant.

Behaviour

There are many books in your local library which will tell you about the scientific study of body language and non-verbal communication. Basically, we are all animals and respond to each other on a simple level in this way. When we meet other animals we need to know that we are not under threat. That is why *smiling* at another human being is such a powerful signal.

When we smile at other people we reassure them that we are not going to attack them, and being smiled at by others is the way *we* receive reassurance that the person facing us is not an enemy. Communication between people is much more relaxed and straightforward when we know we are safe. Think about how difficult it is to make conversation with your dentist before you have treatment! So, to create a good impression, start off the interview on a positive note by entering the room and smiling at all the interviewers present. Even if you are too scared to smile again, you will have started the interview in a confident way. Shaking the hands of those who will be interviewing you is a helpful way to start if you feel confident in doing so. Obviously, if a large table blocks the way between you and a large panel of interviewers, attempting to shake hands may cause more trouble than it will be worth, but if possible, a firm, friendly handshake makes you look open and positive. This applies particularly to women who can make an impact this way through rarity value, as shaking hands is still less common amongst women.

At the end of the interview when you leave, make sure you thank the interviewers for the time and attention you have been afforded and smile again to leave on the same, positive note. If you began by shaking hands, leave the same way.

Eye contact

Looking straight into somebody's eyes when we are talking tells the person that we are interested, attending to what is being said and have nothing to hide. When we feel shy, it is sometimes awkward to keep this direct gaze on the interviewer. If you find this difficult, at least try to look at the interviewer when he or she is asking you a question, even if you look elsewhere during your response. If you are being interviewed by more than one person, do not always try to include all the panel in your glance. Instead, when one inter-viewer asks you an individual question, treat that person as though he or she is the only one interviewing you.

Posture

Other important aspects of body language for an interview are those relating to posture. We can all make ourselves invisible when we wish to and I am sure all my female readers know how to do this. Imagine that you have missed the last bus and have to walk home alone in the dark. What do you do so as not to attract attention?

You hunch your shoulders slightly, look ahead or perhaps down at your feet, walk purposefully but not too fast, and definitely do not meet the eyes of anyone you pass. The look on your face is expressionless and you do not make any noise. You try to cover up as much of yourself as possible with your outer garments to disguise your gender. These tactics will probably work and enable you to look so anonymous that you will reach home untroubled by drunks or trouble-makers.

Now, bearing that example in mind, it should be easy to see how to create the opposite effect when you want to attract attention and be remembered. You must walk tall, pulling yourself up by the head to increase your height and make your spine straight. You will look around you in an alert way and meet any other person's gaze directly, while smiling confidently at everyone you meet.

I hope this illustrates the control we all have over the way we are perceived by other people. In the interview, you do not want to appear insignificant or unremarkable. You want the interview panel to be left with a striking and positive impression of you physically.

When you sit down in the interview, make sure that your bottom is set well back on the seat, with your spine held fairly straight and supported by the back of the chair. Leaning forward slightly gives an impression of keenness. Do not slouch or sprawl in your seat – it implies that you are not taking the interview seriously. Practise in advance to find out which seating position is most comfortable for you. It does not matter whether your legs are crossed or not, but do not keep changing their position or you will distract the interviewer from what you are saying.

Gestures

Hands should be lightly clasped in your lap or can rest on the arms of your chair. Gestures add variety to speech, and your natural style may be to use your hands in this way occasionally. Too much gesticulation implies anxiety and tension, so monitor this when you are practising your answers in front of the mirror.

Confidence

Confidence has been mentioned before as though it should be easy to acquire. Everybody is confident about their abilities in some activity or other. If I asked you to tell me something that you felt confident about, it could be cookery, playing sport or a hobby. If you analyse *why* you are confident at that particular activity, what would you attribute it to? Are you confident because it is a familiar task; because you have been told that you are good at it; because you are well prepared; or because you have studied how to do it?

Often, all these reasons apply, and that is why practising your interview technique is so valuable. Half the terror of an impending interview is because you do not know what to expect. Rehearsing in advance means that you will feel reasssured about which questions may come up, and about your ability to answer them.

Increase your confidence by packing carefully any items you might need if you are going to give a presentation, eg hand–outs or flip-chart pens.

Positive mental attitude

You can also set your own mental attitude to positive instead of negative. Often when going for interviews, candidates are too aware of why they might not be successful. Some of the most common reasons for getting in a negative state of mind are that you feel:

- it is years since you have been tested at an interview;

- you have failed other interviews recently;

- you are desperate to leave your current job;

- you may be too keen to get this job and so feel very worried;

- you may not be really clear what you are looking for;

- you may be deeply demotivated by your career prospects and feel you have nothing to offer.

None of these attitudes will help you to be successful at interview so it is important to convert negative thoughts to more constructive ones. Sports stars claim that the most significant factor in winning is their mental approach to the event. In addition to training and fitness, they need to feel like a winner in order to act like one. We have much more influence over our own thoughts and feelings than you might think. Imagine a day when you are feeling down when out of the blue someone delivers a bouquet of flowers or a present to the door for you. Immediately you feel that your world seems brighter and your mood becomes more positive. This quick change can be brought about by changing the way you are thinking too.

First you need to deliberately concentrate on boosting yourself up. Although we all have disappointments and disasters during our lives, there are also lots of achievements and successes that we can claim.

Spend a few minutes considering each of the following points:

You achieve successfully in several areas of your life already: relationships, keeping your domestic life running, family contacts, holding down a job (if you have one), keeping a nice home going, planning the things you want.

list some more here:

_____

_____

_____

People are impressed by you as an interesting and valuable person: employers who have hired you in the past, family and friends, colleagues, social contacts, lovers and partners.

list some more here:

_____

_____

_____

You can get things when you want to: support from friends, praise from family, attention from loved ones, cooperation from colleagues, being promoted (if you ever have been).

list some more here:

_____

_____

_____

Altogether you are a valuable and interesting person. Still need a bit of convincing? Go out for a walk and think about all the things on this list. Re-visit the best times in your life and what you were doing at the time that made them so good. It was substantially your doing and your personality that helped them to happen. Try and fix an image in your mind of a time or event when you were doing well, so that you can conjure it up again whenever you need to feel good about yourself.

Starting to think about any approaching interview in this frame of mind automatically gives you a head start because you have put your natural doubts to the back of your mind and brought a winning attitude to the fore. When you plan your answers you need to stay in this mind-set and, most importantly, replicate it when you walk into the interview room.

Talk to any high achievers, from supermodels to corporate leaders, and they will all say that they have their private worries and stresses, but that they incorporate a positive vision of what they want to achieve and then concentrate on how they can get it to focus them on success. This kind of mental exercise can work just as well for you too.

The journey

The journey to the interview can be a source of anxiety. Plan in advance how much time to allow. If possible, do a 'dummy' or practice run and make sure that you can find the right building and the correct entrance to use. Allow extra time for unforeseen hold-ups. It is important to be on time for your interview, so plan to arrive 15 minutes early. If you are delayed for any reason, telephone to let the company know and inform them of your expected time of arrival – although if you arrive too late you may miss the chance of being interviewed altogether. Remember that *everybody* you talk to at the company may be asked for their opinion of you – including the secretary or receptionist at the front door, the porter and the person who brings you your cup of coffee. I know of a candidate who was only successful because he was friendly and chatty to the office administrator whilst waiting to go in to his interview. The panel could not decide between two equally ranked candidates. They gave the casting vote to someone who had met both – yes, the office administrator.

Voice

Interview nerves affect people in different ways. Some people speak very softly, some talk too fast and start gabbling, others become hesitant and leave long gaps between words. Some people stammer under pressure and some just answer briefly, replying 'yes' or 'no' whenever possible, rather than speaking up about themselves. None of these responses is helpful in an interview.

We have already noted that the whole purpose of your being invited along is for the interviewer to find out as much as possible about you in the time available. Short, quiet, babbled or hesitant answers will not suffice. Of course, any experienced interviewer will make allowances for initial nerves, but will expect you to settle down to the task in hand fairly quickly.

Just try to imagine that you are talking to someone you know fairly well, and speak in a relaxed and easy manner. Normally, the longer you worry about getting every word and phrase exactly right, the more tangled up you become. Pauses sound fine as part of ordinary speech and are preferable to 'ums' and 'ers'. Pauses only become a problem if they are excessively long, in which case an interviewer may not realise when you have finished speaking. If you know that you are prone to leaving such gaps in the conversation, you could mark the end of your answer by saying something like: 'Those are the main points that I want to make.'

Many of us speak with a regional accent of some kind. It is one of the things about ourselves that we cannot change, or at least not without a great deal of effort. Do not feel self-conscious about the way you speak. It is part of who you are. However, if you are worried that your accent may mean that you are not understood in interviews, try to enunciate clearly, speak slowly and limit your use of local words and phrases whose meaning will not be clear outside your own community.

Controlling nerves

Everybody suffers from nervousness in situations which create anxiety. Some of our greatest actors are literally sick before each and every performance, showing that the energy which is generated by nervous tension is crucial to giving a good performance. The trick is to make this tension work *for* you rather than against you.

When we are nervous the body reacts to the fact that the forthcoming event is important to us. We have spent time and trouble rehearsing for the interview and the body is getting its response mechanism ready either to fight or run away. This flight or fight mechanism is a throw-back to the times when we had to act in one of these ways to survive. We need to harness these nerves to make us fight, or at least act impressively before the interviewer, rather than panic and dry up. When your nerves work for you, you feel extra alive, highly conscious of everything that is going on around you, very focussed on the task in hand and excited by the prospect of the performance ahead.

In your life there will be many occasions which will bring on an attack of nerves, and knowing how to control it will come in useful. The main thing is to have some long-term goal to concentrate on and carry you through the experience. Like the actors who force themselves on stage because the show must go on, you can talk and impress people despite your nerves if you keep the purpose of the interview at the front of your mind all the time.

You have been invited to this interview so that the employer can find out about you, and you are going to tell the interviewer all about yourself. If you have prepared well for the interview, you will have thought through how your experience ties in with what the employer is looking for and you will feel excited and enthusiastic about the idea of what you can contribute to the organisation.

This energy you have generated will carry you through the interview, and all the interviewer will remember about you will be your keenness and enthusiasm for the position rather than your nerves.

I once interviewed a series of people for a job requiring energy and commitment. Each one seemed competent and suitable, but none stood out. At the end of the last interview, the candidate said goodbye with the words: 'I would really love doing this job, you know.' Her obvious enthusiasm shone through her nervousness and I offered her the job on the spot, confident that she was the most suitable candidate. Showing enthusiasm does not mean being immature or sounding desperate to get a job. It requires a genuinely positive attitude to the challenges and opportunities that the vacancy offers.

Your nervousness does not show to other people as much as you think. I run workshops to prepare people for interviews where I make everybody do a mock interview in front of the whole group. Every single person admits to being terribly nervous, but the audience is always amazed that each interviewee seems calms and collected. Nerves just do not show. We may know that our palms are sweaty, our stomachs churning and our knees knocking, but no one else will realise our predicament.

When an attack of nerves strikes, the energy generated often escapes in repetitive gestures or mannerisms. Fidgeting with coins in a pocket, twiddling strands of hair, constantly touching face or mouth are just some of the ways in which we show our nervousness and we are often unaware of such habits.

A good way to learn about nervous mannerisms is to ask yourself some of the practice questions which start on page 67, whilst watching your reflection in a mirror. This is your chance to see yourself as others see you. Alternatively, you could ask a friend or relative to give you some honest feedback on your behaviour under pressure. Hands are best kept under control, clasped lightly together in your lap.

The interviewer may also be experiencing some feelings of nervousness. Many managers have little experience or skill at conducting interviews. It is still rare for interviewers to have had any training for the role, particularly in small companies. Most of these employers just muddle through, trying to use common sense in a difficult situation. Moreover, in a panel interview there may be all sorts of tension between the representative from the personnel department, the line manager and the other members of the group of which you will not be aware.

Imagine that you have been asked to interview some job candidates. How would you feel? Perhaps a little apprehensive in advance and on the shaky side when the very first candidate comes into the room? You have never met this person before. Would you be totally confident about what to say and how to handle the candidates? Interviewing is a difficult task because it is stressful to be faced with someone whom we have to talk to in some depth but do not know.

It is comforting to know that most interviewers are nervous. An interview can be a disquieting experience for the people on both sides of the table. Obviously, the interviewer has a relatively more powerful position than the interviewee – he or she has a job to offer – but it is important to remember all the dynamics of the occasion.

Make sure that you visit the toilet before the interview and do not drink or take drugs to calm you down. Both will impair your performance, and alcohol can always be smelt on the breath.

Relaxation exercises

Breathing exercise

Breathing exercises are one way of managing feelings of nervousness. When we are under strain our breathing is likely to become shallow, and we do not use all our lung capacity. The effect is to starve the brain of the vital oxygen it needs in order to think quickly and clearly. To counteract this, just before you enter the interview room, take several deep breaths.

This exercise is easiest to do when standing. Inhale slowly, breathing through your nose, and try to fill your lungs completely. After a count of three, slowly exhale through your mouth. Concentrate on expelling all the air that you took in. Feel your shoulders relax as you breathe out. Repeat this deep breathing four or five times.

You should see your stomach move out with each breath in, and flatten each time you breathe out. Do not take this exercise too far – hyperventilation is not necessary! The exercise should be carried out only in a gentle and rhythmic manner. If it is impossible to have some time on your own, with practice you should be able to breathe deeply without anyone noticing.

Facial exercise

Smiling has another benefit apart from putting the interviewer at ease. It is also an effective way of exercising your facial muscles. When we tense up, our faces can take on a stony expression and a frown of concentration. To relax your face, gently say all the vowel sounds a, e, i, o, u, and stretch your mouth in an exaggerated manner to make all your facial muscles flex. Repeat the exercise several times.

Finish off with a big, wide grin. Make sure that you are not being watched while doing this exercise in case you frighten the other candidates!

To control your feelings of nervousness

1. Feel determined about what you want to say.

2. Keep in the forefront of your mind what you want to achieve.

3. Remember to do some deep breathing, the facial exercise a-e-i-o-u and to *smile*.

4. Remember that nerves never show as much as you think.

5. Bear in mind that the interviewer is probably under some strain too.

Dos and don'ts

Do   keep focussed.

Do   check your appearance before you enter.

Do   wear smart but comfortable clothes.

Don't   fidget, try to sit calmly.

Don't   talk too fast because of nerves, pause often.

Don't   take your worries into the interview – go in ready to shine.

Answering interview questions

Examples of interview questions and answers

The longest part of any job interview tends to be the questions asked of the candidate. It is also the cause of most stress. We worry whether we will be able to answer the questions convincingly; whether anything will come up to catch us out and if our answers are as impressive as those of the other candidates. It is the case that the more we know in advance about the questions to be asked, the more comprehensive our preparation and the more confident our delivery on the day. Whilst it is impossible to accurately predict every single question that will be asked in an interview, we can guesstimate most of the likely areas to be covered.

Think about the questions from the employer's point of view. He or she only has a limited time to come to a decision about which is the best candidate from those on the shortlist. If all candidates are to be asked the same or similar questions so that their answers can be compared and contrasted together, there needs to be a list of questions prepared and ready to ask in advance of the interview. If a job description and personnel specification exist for the post, these will form the basis of a lot of the questioning. If the employer has taken the trouble to be explicit in advance about what will be done in the job and the essential and desirable qualities required for the job, these lists provide a likely direction for questioning in the interview.

The employer is likely to start with questions that explore the backgrounds of the candidates, frequently covering education, training and experience. Most interviewers like to ask about any interests or hobbies that the candidates may have, to find out what kind of person they are outside, as well as inside, the workplace. More general questions will follow about attitudes, aptitudes and abilities plus perhaps some exploration of any ideas the candidates have about how they would approach carrying out the job on offer. For more senior or specialised roles, there may well be some questions designed to see if the candidates have a vision of how they would develop the role, if appointed.

Here is a selection of typical questions that you may be asked in an interview. Following each question are some suggestions about the type of information that the interviewer would be interested in as part of your answer. You will rarely be asked *all* these questions, and some may not apply to you, but as full a range as possible has been included to give you practice at how to respond. If you can answer all these questions confidently you are truly ready for your interview. Read each question, then covering up my guidelines underneath, try to answer as if you were in an interview. Then read my comments and see if there is anything you would subsequently alter about the answer you gave.

You will see that a full answer for each question has been suggested. You are only being asked these questions to prompt you to talk about yourself. The more information you can give, the more helpful it will be, so long as your answers are concise, clear and relevant. Details are not as important as stressing what skills or experience you have gained.

Many people feel that they should not repeat information that they have already given on their CV or application form for fear of sounding repetitive and boring to the interviewer. This is a mistaken view. Any paper application that you made would have been considered along with several, if not many others. It may have been read in a hurry and not been looked at since. It is unlikely that much will be remembered and even if it is, it does not hurt to reiterate how good a candidate for this vacancy you really are.

Education and training

1. Why did you decide to go to college?
This requires a full answer, and you need to go back to when you left school in order to be able to answer it. What were your long-term ambitions at the time? Were there certain subjects you particularly enjoyed at school and wished to continue to study? How and why did you choose your particular course and your specialist subjects?

Perhaps you studied as a mature student. What factors led to your decision to return to learning in this way? The employer will be interested in your motivation. It is important to show that you did not just drift into attending college on the academic conveyor belt but that you made your own clear choices along the way.

2. Can you tell me about your college course?
This kind of open question about any education or training you have completed invites you to make connections that can impress your interviewer. For instance, were there any aspects of your college course that could have a direct bearing on the job for which you are being interviewed? Do you feel that you learned more from one part of the course

than another? Were there any extra-mural or external
activities that you took part in that now have any relevance
to this vacancy?

Many people forget to explain exactly where they went to
college and precisely which course they took. Even if the
employer already has this information on your CV or application form, he or she may not have it to hand, or even
remember having seen it before. What sort of teaching
methods were employed? Were there compulsory core
subjects and specialist options? How did you decide which
to study?

3. Did you enjoy any particular part of your studies more than the rest?

This question gives you the chance to show some enthusiasm. Even if you struggled through college, dropped out of
the course early or did less well than you expected, there
must be some aspect of the experience that you can discuss
here. Try and find an example that links with the job you are
applying for. Perhaps if you were being interviewed for a
sales vacancy you could say: 'In my second year and above
we were asked to talk to potential students each year. I
enjoyed explaining the course to them, answering their questions and giving them advice about their application. I felt
like an ambassador for the college at those times.'

The employer is trying to find out what sort of person you
are to get clues about the sort of work that would suit you
best. Was there some particular option or course that you
enjoyed more than others? Did it involve working alone or
with other people?

Think about the impression you will create with particular
answers. Talking at length about how much you enjoyed
researching alone in the chemistry laboratory at college will
indicate your preferred style of working. The interviewer will
probably assume that you are not the team player that he or
she is looking for.

4. Can you tell me about a project that you worked on at school or college?

Working life is full of dealing with projects of one kind or another, from getting a letter typed, to managing a building contract, to supervising a team of accounts clerks. This question is being asked because the answer will give an indication of the way you would deal with this kind of work. You will need to explain how the project was conceived, what the task was, who else was involved in the work, how you worked together, how you handled any difficulties, your particular contribution and what you think you gained from the exercise.

Were there any particular issues in the management of the project that were significant? What helped or hindered at the planning stage? Did everything go according to plan?

Employment history

5. Have you had any work experience?

This question is often asked of younger people who have just left full-time education. No employer wants to hear that you are completely inexperienced, even if you only left college a week ago. You will need to come up with some kind of answer in order to reassure the interviewer that you are used to the routine of work, that you can hold down a position and that someone else has wanted to employ you in the past. Perhaps you have done a paper round; worked on voluntary projects while at school; had holiday or vacation jobs or participated in a work experience programme at school?

If you have never done any type of work at all, do not let this situation continue as now is the time to start. You could offer your services to a community organisation on a voluntary basis or 'work shadow' some friend or relative who does what you are interested in. A training course could help you pick up many transferable skills. If you are studying it may be possible to get a Saturday or evening job. Apart from providing you with a positive response to this question, and giving you added purpose and contacts, the work experience may gain you a character reference from the organisation concerned.

6. Can you tell me about your last job?

First you need to summarise the main features of your last job so that your interviewer can quickly and easily understand what you were doing, why and how. Forget that you have already written about this in your CV or application form. Imagine this is the first time you have discussed the job. Think through in advance what aspects of the job will be impressive to this employer and stress how you have learned about these areas in particular. It is not the precise details of what you were doing in the job that are wanted, but an account of the main skills involved and what you contributed to the organisation. Give concrete examples where possible to illustrate your points and stress how you progressed in the course of the job.

7. Why did you leave your last position?

This is not the time to decry either your last job, the people you worked with or the employer concerned. A candidate who appears to have difficulty in getting on with people will definitely not be offered the position. Nobody wants to risk employing a trouble-maker. You will need to provide positive reasons for moving on from your last job, either involving different work or preferably taking up a new opportunity – to study, do voluntary work, or whatever you say you have been doing since you stopped work. If there were major problems in your last (or present) job that you wish to mention, you should only talk about possible improvements which could be made in order to sound upbeat.

If you had a terrible time in your last job and feel that nothing good happened to you there, try looking back at the experience now. With hindsight you may be able to describe some learning points for you personally, aspects of your time there that did teach you about the world of work in a positive manner or motivating factors to leave that could seem useful to the interviewer. For instance: you felt that you wanted a role with more responsibility, greater challenges or more scope to be creative.

If you are currently employed, make sure that you do not sound desperate to escape from your job. You must provide illustrations of the way you could contribute to the position for which you have applied.

8. What have you been doing since you left your last job?
This is a good question which you can easily use to your advantage. If you are not working, and even if you have been unemployed for some time, you must come up with something positive that you have been doing with your time since you last worked. It is not enough to say that you have been looking for another job – that will be assumed.

The best answer will be either that you have been doing some sort of course to improve your skills or that you have been doing some voluntary work. If you know someone who runs a business, it may be possible to say that you have been doing some freelance contract work, helping out with this company.

Whatever you say will need to be backed up with details of your activities if the employer wishes to know more. If you are not doing anything with your time – you must start something immediately. Apart from being an absolute necessity for your CV and job applications, it is the perfect antidote to the depression that can come with unemployment. Contact your local volunteer bureau to see what opportunities are available in your area.

9. What has been your greatest achievement in your working history?
Some hard thinking before the interview is needed in order to answer this question. The example that you choose should

convey some of the principal qualities needed in the job applied for and should be explained clearly and concisely. A useful way to make sure you don't ramble is to structure your answer into three key points. The first point could cover what the achievement was, the second could explain the circumstances or the background and the third point could explain why you feel that this represents the greatest achievement in your work to date.

10. Can you tell me about a problem that you have had to deal with?

The point of this question, as far as the employer is concerned, is to see how you would tackle obstacles at work. An ideal answer would involve you in thinking through a difficulty and solving it with the help of other people. If you can indicate some general lessons that you learnt from the experience, so much the better. Please do not volunteer an answer that makes you look as though you could not deal with the problem! Make sure you choose something that shows your role to be positive, practical and ultimately successful. If you worked with other people to solve the problem, had to communicate clearly and learned something from the experience, so much the better. It could involve dealing with difficult customers, a mix-up of resources, rescuing an organisational mess, in fact anything where your role has had a major effect for the good.

11. What would you do if you had a problem that you could not deal with? Perhaps you are faced with a difficult customer.

This question is being asked to assess your ability to handle customers and provide them with the best care you can. Everybody has to ask for help at times during their working life. Your answer should show that you would not give up as soon as you were faced with a problem, such as an irate or awkward customer. The employer wants to see that you would be responsible and calm in your dealings with customers. Explain that you would try to find out the exact nature of the problem troubling the person, while calming him or her down, if necessary. You need to apologise quickly in cases like this. Apologising does not mean taking all of the blame – you can feel sorry that the customer feels upset and show empathy. It can really diffuse the tension. In many cases you would be able to sort out the problem yourself, but sometimes the issue needs to be dealt with at a higher level.

Tell the interviewer that you are aware that if this were the case you would need all the details in order to pass them on to whoever could sort out the problem. Apologising to the customer for the delay, you would tell him or her exactly when the problem would be attended to. You would then pass on the query to your supervisor or the person responsible.

12. Which of all your jobs have you found the most interesting, and why?

It is easy to hear a question like this and yet forget to answer the second part of the question. You need not only to have the most interesting job to talk about but also be ready to explain clearly exactly what was so interesting about it. This question may be asked if you have had a varied employment history. A wise answer would include work similar to the job on offer to show that you will be happy and involved in your work. Try to justify your choice by giving examples of your main achievements in the time spent there, or explaining the particularly interesting aspects.

13. What are the most satisfying and the most frustrating aspects of your present/last job?

You may be asked this question to find out what you like best and least about your most recent position. Think carefully before you phrase your answer. The most satisfying aspects of the job should be those most closely linked to the position that you are now applying for. A long list of frustrations can make you sound like a moaner. If there was some particularly difficult aspect of the job, try to say how you helped to improve it. If at the time you did not, or could not rectify it, can you think of remedies now that might work? Make sure the frustrations are not also present in the job you are applying for now.

Interests

14. What hobbies or interests do you have?

Why should employers be interested in the answer to this question? Is it pure nosiness? Everything you say about yourself contributes to the general impression gained about you. If I tell you that my hobbies are knitting, cookery, needlework, decorating cakes and bird-watching, you have an idea of the sort of person I am. If, however, I tell you that my hobbies include karate, African music, organising a community group, gardening and swimming, the picture is quite different.

You need to think hard about which hobbies and interests to mention. They can illustrate that you have a well-rounded personality and lead a full and satisfying life. Examples of times when you were in a leading or organising role will create a good impression.

There are some interests that we all have in common and these are not worth listing. We all read, watch television and socialise with other people, and these activities should not be part of your answer unless you have something specific to say about them. Be warned that if you mention them, you are likely to be asked either 'What was the last book you read?' or 'Can you tell me about a television programme that inter-ested you lately?' Details of the latest episode of your favourite soap opera will not suffice!

Do not be too specific about any political or religious interests unless they are of direct relevance to the job in question. It is better just to say, as in the example above, that you are actively involved in the local community. The interviewer may hold different views from your own.

You do not have to spend time on all the hobbies that you mention, but be sure that you know enough to talk about the subject in some depth. Employers often pick on hobbies as an easy area of questioning and will be interested in discussing more unusual choices.

You should have some knowledge of every hobby that you mention, even if you need to say: 'Well, I am very interested in windsurfing. At the moment I am finding out about it, but I intend to spend some time next summer having a go,' or 'I used to play a lot of basketball at school. I'm a bit rusty now, but I watch it when I can and am joining an evening class shortly to brush up my skills.'

The three points to be aware of when answering this question are:

- Include a variety of interests – some using your mind and some sporting or physical activities to show that you are a lively, healthy and active person. Try to have at least one practical interest and one which uses your mental aptitudes.

- Ensure that you have at least one pastime which is different from other people's. This makes it easier for employers to ask you follow-up questions and to remember you subsequently.

- Be prepared to discuss any of the topics you mention in some detail.

General

15. What are your strengths?
This is one of my favourite questions. If you were ever given a chance to shine – this is it. Although at first sight this seems daunting, it is easy to prepare an impressive answer if you consider it before the interview.

In the space below make a list of ten of your good qualities. Each point should comprise one word or short phrase and should relate to your behaviour at work.

Examples could be: 'Flexible; good at keeping to deadlines; calm; can work under pressure ...' Everybody's list will be different. If you find this exercise difficult, try to imagine what your mother, your best friend, your dog – or whoever loves you most in the world – would say about you if they were describing your best characteristics to a stranger.

YOUR TEN STRENGTHS

1. _____

2. _____

3. _____

4. _____

5. _____

6. _____

7. _____

8. _____

9. _____

10. _____

This list is very useful as the basis for answering any question about your strengths. By selecting five or six points from your list, you can put together a clear and powerful answer. Because you have prepared in advance, you will sound confident about your own abilities and proud of your character.

Most people find it hard to compile the list of their ten strengths, and even harder to talk about them in an interview. Do not worry about sounding boastful. It is much more common for candidates to be too modest than to blow their own trumpets. I recommend that you don't hold back from explaining just how good you are in this answer.

The list of ten points can be kept and added to throughout your life. Whenever a colleague or friend compliments you on some aspect of your character, add it to your list. It will prove useful when you have to complete a CV, application form or go for interviews in the future, as well as providing a boost to your confidence when you need one!

16. What are your weaknesses?

Whatever does the employer mean by asking this question? Nobody will want to employ someone who can reel off a long list of serious faults. The best way to answer is not to admit to any weaknesses at all. If you do mention weaknesses, make sure that they are those which sound more like strengths. For instance: 'I sometimes take my work too seriously and will stay late at the office to get something finished', or 'I tend to be very flexible as a work colleague, and I will do the jobs that no one else wants to do'. No employer will mind you having weaknesses like these!

17. What are you most proud of?

This should normally relate to some work experience, and it is helpful if it can demonstrate the necessary qualities for the job on offer. Any project or team work where you played a significant role could be mentioned. Any instance where your contribution made a real difference, where you tried an innovative approach or learnt something new would be well worth mentioning.

18. Which current affairs problem have you been aware of lately?

This is a favourite question for public service jobs and is designed to check two things. The first is that your understanding of the world is wide and up to date, and the second is to see what sort of political attitudes you have. It therefore makes sense to read a quality daily newspaper thoroughly for at least a week before any interview. This is particularly relevant when you have applied for a job where you would be representing the views of the employing organisation.

Employers rarely want candidates to express strong political views in interviews. This is certainly true of the Civil Service, voluntary sector and local authorities. Ideally, you should illustrate that you know about a current issue in some depth, you are aware of the two sides to the argument, you can understand the feelings on both sides, and you realise what a difficult political problem it is.

Politics should be left to politicians, or to any of us in our private lives, not brought into the workplace. If you are asked for your opinion on a political issue, refrain from coming down heavily on either side. Government or local authority employers want to be sure that you are aware of the need to put into practice the wishes of the political masters of the day – and they can be right or left wing.

19. What do you see yourself doing in five years' time?

This is a similar question to one about your career ambitions. Think – why is the employer asking this? Does he or she want to know that you plan to train as an accountant or an actor in your spare time, and leave this job as soon as possible? No. He or she wants a member of staff who is serious about the vacancy and interested in staying put for a considerable time. Your answer could indicate that you hope to be in the company, but perhaps with greater responsibilities. Not everyone is seeking promotion. You could say that you would be interested in gaining a more specialist role.

20. Why should we employ you rather than another candidate?

This is another good question as it enables you to use your list of ten strengths again. (See question 15 above.)

Employers are interested in hearing about your skills, experience and personality.

In your answer you could mention any of your particular skills which relate to the job, your relevant experience, and add those aspects of your personality which best suit you for the position. A question like this is a gift to an interviewee. Do not be worried about boasting. This is the time to 'sell yourself' strongly to the interviewer. You are being asked to summarise your application – and the answer to this question is the crux of the whole interview.

You can bring in your ideas here – explain the thoughts you have had about the organisation and your vision for the future of the job. The more senior the position that you are applying for, the more likely it is that no-one on the panel knows exactly what they are looking for when recruiting. By definition, the more rare or specialised the role, the fewer people there will be who fully understand how the job could or should be done. In addition, the more significant the position for the organisation, the more important it will be to have it filled by someone with ideas and initiative. You can show that you will bring added value to the job in comparison with the other candidates by sharing your view of the way the job should be carried out. This does require you to have spent some serious thinking time considering the job, the situation of the organisation and the possibilities of the role.

21. What other careers are you interested in?
If you are applying for a computer operator's job in order to pay the rent and secretly want to be a police officer or a ballet dancer, keep that to yourself. Again, think – why is the employer interested in this question? He or she will be most impressed by the candidate who seems serious about the job on offer and about making a career in this line of work. Imply that your career ambitions are in this exact field. You could add that in the future you would be interested in

working your way up to a position with more responsibility, or perhaps specialising in a particular area of the work.

22. Which other organisations have you applied to?

This question is similar to the one above. The employer does not want a candidate whom every other company has rejected. You want to convey the impression that you feel this particular vacancy is exactly the right one for you, and you have been saving yourself for it. I recommend that you say you are being choosy about the companies you approach. In other words, imply that you have not found such an interesting vacancy as this before, and say why.

23. What does equal opportunities mean to you?

This is the most difficult question to answer. But, fortunately, most interviewers are not too sure what the correct answer is. As long as you demonstrate that you understand the importance of everyone getting the same chances in employment and access to services, the employer will be impressed.

Many people answer: 'Treating everyone in the same way.' I think this answer is a little too simple. Some people with special needs may need extra help. For instance, someone with a visual impairment may need special facilities or aids in order to do their job properly. You may have some personal awareness of this subject and feel like expressing it in the interview. For instance: 'As a woman, I know how it feels not to be taken seriously sometimes, so I always try to make sure that I treat everyone with respect,' or 'When I first arrived in this country I felt like an outsider and I am keen to help those who may need more support to make full use of the services offered by this organisation.'

24. How would you put equal opportunities into practice?

This is often asked together with the previous question. The trick here is to think about the best answer in the light of the organisation applied to. Why has the employer decided to ask you this? It is likely that the current vacancy is with a large organisation, public company or local authority which is looking for staff who will be aware of two things: first, that services need to be made available to the whole population and, second, that colleagues may need support and understanding too. Explain how you would aim to fulfil these requirements in that job.

The vacancy

25. Tell me what you know about this organisation.
There is no excuse for not having a response to this question. Whatever the particular job that you are applying for, the interviewer will expect you to have some knowledge of the organisation, and the more the better. Whether you have seen an advertisement, been sent a job description or person specification or read literature about the company, you should have some information to offer. The more you know, the more suitable you will seem.

Search the Internet for any information that may exist. First look up the name of the organisation using a search engine. Most medium to large organisations now have a Web site which outlines their main business, gives details of current priorities and past endeavours. If you can find nothing on the company directly, try looking up a competitor or reading about the sector in which the company is based. If you do not have your own computer facilities, try the local library. They will have helpful and knowledgeable staff who will help you and many reference materials, printed and computerised, that they can introduce you to.

If you have found no prior information then at least use your eyes and ears in the interview. Are there brochures or posters in evidence; how do the staff seem to relate to each other and outsiders, what first impressions have you gained?

Get talking to reception staff about how they find working there. Sharing your thoughts on these topics, always stressing positive points, will show you are alert and interested.

26. Why do you want to work for this company?
Answering this question depends on the type of work offered and how much you know about the company concerned. You need to stress the particular type of organisation in relation to your own skills, strengths and personality. Your ideas about what you would do if offered the job are worth contributing here. Try to make the case for a good match between the company's aims and outlook and your own.

27. If you were offered this job, how do you think you would spend your first two weeks with the company?
This is a more general question designed to check that you have a realistic and sensible approach to work. In most jobs, unless you have worked for the organisation before, you need to spend your first few days getting used to the new environment. This means finding your way around, meeting your new colleagues, and familiarising yourself with the rules and working practices. You would also probably spend some time with your new manager learning how the work is done and about current priorities.

28. What do you think are the most important issues facing this organisation at the moment?
This question may well be posed when certain political or financial issues affect an organisation. Examples of such organisations could be charities, voluntary organisations or local authorities. Your answer would depend on the exact nature of the employer, but could include: generating income; allocating scarce resources; setting objectives; implementing cutbacks; quality control; managing grant-funding or some particular campaign with which the organisation is involved.

You will really have to do your homework though in order to answer this convincingly. Can you find out what the press profile of the organisation has been lately? Visit a Web site such as www.guardian.co.uk and search for recent news about them. That may tell you about their priorities and concerns.

29. What do you think you can contribute to this company?

This is one of my favourite questions. As far as an employer is concerned, this represents the crux of the whole interview. This is your chance to shine, by saying exactly why you decided to apply for the job. You will need to bring out your particular strengths and show clearly what you can offer. Quoting your experience and skills will help to impress on the employer that you will be a valuable addition to the team. Don't forget to include good points about your personality here. Move on to explain how you would use all these things to help build on the success of the organisation.

30. Why are you applying for the post?

This is another variant on the last question and should be answered in the same way. Try to structure your answers. Give three key points such as:

1. my skills and experience;

2. my character and personality;

3. my vision for this particular post.

In this way you will give a clearer response while still including everything you need to say.

Dos and don'ts

Do   let go! Interviewers want to get to know who you are, so feel free to be yourself. Then if they don't want you for the job, that may be for the best as you may not have fitted in.

Do	mind the gap! Make a positive statement about things that would otherwise look negative.
Do	speak up for yourself – you have nothing to lose and everything to gain. Think of the interview as a kind of performance, you need to be a bit 'larger than life'.
Do	take care with your appearance; consider every aspect of your presentation.
Do	keep your answers simple and clear.
Do	speak as you would normally; there is no need to put on an act by using long words or complicated sentences.
Do	boast about your strengths and achievements – all the other candidates will be trying to make themselves look extra good too.
Don't	lose your confidence; concentrate on the vacancy that you are interested in.
Don't	worry about nerves – they never show to other people as much as you think they do.
Don't	smoke or drink tea or coffee in the interview.
Don't	assume that the interviewer knows what you are talking about – the things that you think are obvious may be unclear to others.
Don't	ever give just 'yes' or 'no' answers – the employer will want to know more than that.
Don't	use jargon or specialised terms without an explanation.
Don't	lie about yourself – you could face dismissal if you obtain a job under false pretences.

Dealing with tricky situations

Starting off the interview

I recommend shaking hands with the interviewer when you enter the room; it shows that you are keen to meet him or her and able to be formally polite. Women sometimes find this difficult, as shaking hands has in the past been more of a male habit. Do not worry if you feel that it would be beyond your capabilities, in a nervous state, to walk in and confidently grasp a stranger's hand, but do respond positively if the interviewer wants to greet you in this way.

You will normally be invited to sit down but, if the interviewer does not mention it, do not immediately assume that he or she is playing some fiendish trick to see how you react under pressure. The much more likely explanation is that he or she has simply forgotten to invite you to be seated, in their concern about which question to ask you first. The solution is to smile and ask politely: 'May I sit down?'

Good manners

On the subject of politeness, you can never be too polite in interviews. On leaving I recommend saying: 'Thank you very much for your time. I have enjoyed meeting you. Goodbye.' Even if you are a habitual smoker, resist the temptation at the interview. Falling ash and smoke surrounding the interviewee never look impressive, even if the employer is smoking.

Some people feel that if they are offered tea or coffee, it is impolite to refuse. But it is best *not* to accept. In my personal experience, nervousness only leads to disasters such as the cup falling on the floor or the drink filling the saucer or splashing on your interview suit. Have a strong cup of coffee after the interview is safely over.

If you do not understand or hear a question properly, do not panic. Just ask the questioner to repeat the question. It is better to do this than guess at what was said and make a mistake.

The interview does not go as planned

If you have planned your responses but do not have the chance to get your points across, you can sometimes hijack the interview so that it goes more in your favour. Suppose that you had not been asked about your strengths, and want to bring in some of the points from your list of ten characteristics. At the end of the interview you could say: 'I would just like to add a brief comment about the sort of person I am' and then say your piece.

Panic sets in

Even the most well-prepared candidate can suffer from temporary drying-up in mid-interview. If your mind goes blank, breathe deeply and play for time by saying something like: 'That's an interesting question.' This allows you a few extra seconds to collect your thoughts. If you are really stuck, ask if you could return to that question later in the interview. Similarly, if you dry-up mid-answer, the situation can be retrieved. Just say, 'I'm sorry, I've just lost the thread for a minute. Could you repeat the question please?'

Don't know the answer?

Occasionally, you may be faced with a question that is just too difficult. If you cannot think of anything to say on a subject, explain so simply and without being embarrassed. If possible, indicate that it is an area you are keen to explore and learn more about in the future. Afterwards, do not let it worry you, but move on to the next question, clear that you are doing the best you can.

Interviewer seems uninterested

Sometimes you can meet an interviewer who seems switched off or bored as soon as you start talking. This is very unprofessional behaviour on their part and you should not let it put you off. Keep to your planned answers and try to make eye contact as much as possible. Do not assume it means bad news for your prospects. He or she may just be tired, under strain or just always have that expression on their face!

Money

Most jobs give some indication of the salary or wages in the advertisement or job details. If money is not mentioned, avoid discussing the subject at the interview. You will obviously not take any job without knowing what you are going to be paid, but you can always check on this when the interview is over. If you are offered the job, you can say: 'I'm certainly interested in the position, but haven't yet had full details about the conditions of employment. Perhaps you could tell me the salary for the job?'

Having to negotiate your own salary

Some jobs, particularly in sales, do not have a fixed salary to offer. They set pay individually as a result of a negotiation with the candidate after a job offer has been made. You will normally know if this is the case as there will be no salary details available on advert or job details. Being forewarned means that you can think through your position prior to having to discuss it.

Start by working out exactly how much you need to earn. What is the lowest salary that you can afford to earn and still survive and maintain the lowest standard of living that you are prepared to accept?

Next what is the maximum that you could expect? Look carefully at the equivalent salaries available to see what the range covers. These two totals represent your lower and upper limits within which you can negotiate. Keep these figures to yourself, as they represent your own private calculations which should not be divulged. Any offer lower than your minimum should be rejected as impossible or unpleasant to live on. Any offer lower than your maximum amount, you should try to increase nearer to the maximum.

You may well be asked about your current pay level. Make sure you represent the whole package including any perks, overtime or bonuses that you regularly receive. If asked to say what salary you are expecting, you can quote the current package and say that you would want to be improving on that level. Stay enthusiastic about the job whilst in these negotiations and talk about what you think you are worth because of the contribution you can make to the role. Maintaining a position often works. When the employer is really not going to go any higher and says that it is their final offer, you need to see where such an amount comes in your limits before deciding. Remember not to be too rigid on pay though. If the job is really interesting, you may be better off accepting lower pay for better prospects in the longer run.

Points to remember

1. Take a minute before you answer each question to group your thoughts together clearly in your mind, as if you were giving a mini-presentation each time.

2. Try really hard to put everything relevant forward, this is your big chance.

3. Show enthusiasm where you can, everyone wants someone keen to work with.

4. If you feel you have not said all you could, ask if you can add a summary at the end.

Bringing it all together

Step-by-step checklist

Step 1. Planning

In order to feel confident you need to plan how to convince the employer that you are the best candidate for the position. Be familiar with the job that you will be interviewed for. Collect any helpful information about the company. Go over your application for the post and carefully analyse the specific vacancy to see what the employer is looking for. The successful candidate will have brought out in the interview those examples of his or her background, skills and personality which complement the ones required for the position. Think about the possible challenges and opportunities of the post to give you a picture of what you would do once offered the position.

The most important point to convey is that you are the right type of person for the job. Study your list of ten character strengths (see page 76). Select which will be the most useful at the interview. Construct sentences using the points that you have chosen, giving examples of the relevant type of behaviour. The details of previous experiences are not as important as your main achievements, the transferable skills learned or the way in which you behaved.

Mind the gap! Gaps can be literally breaks in your employment history or events that you need to convey in a positive light. You need to ensure that you do not sound apologetic about your experiences but can illustrate what you have learned from them. The most important thing about your answers is that they should all be positive – about your previous experience, your skills and strengths, and what makes you right for this particular job.

You can plan your journey in advance; allow extra time to ensure that you arrive at least 15 minutes early for your appointment. There is also some planning work to be done on your physical presentation. Decide which clothes to wear, concentrating on the most flattering style and colours for you. Take professional advice if necessary – a visit to an image consultant can be great fun.

Step 2. Preparation

You need to prepare yourself thoroughly for the interview. Do a dummy run of the journey to the organisation concerned if it is in an unfamiliar area. A vital part of your preparation concerns the clothes you will wear. They should all be clean, well ironed and look immaculate. Have a bath and wash your hair before the interview. Give due consideration to your accessories which can contribute to the employer's important first impression of you.

The most vital aspect of the preparatory stage is to speak aloud the answers that you have planned. This rehearses you for the actual performance and increases your confidence when you are asked the questions for real. Think what the interviewer is going to want to hear from you. You must sound keen and interested in the job; be someone with the right skills or be trainable, and show that you can fit into the organisation.

When you are practising your answers with a friend or in front of the mirror, be aware of how you look and sound. Your voice should be steady and clear. Try to smile while you are talking and see how it improves the way you look. Rehearse your walk; holding yourself up straight can reinforce the impression of confidence as well as making it easier to breathe.

Step 3. Generating confidence

This is the time to let your enthusiasm show. One of the most attractive attributes in a job candidate is a genuine interest in the work. Do not worry about your nerves – just concentrate on enjoying the interview. You are well prepared and confident that you are the right candidate for the job, and you can look forward to meeting the employer and telling him or her about yourself.

Before the event itself, relax your face with the exercise on page 62 and take some deep breaths. Walk in with your head held up, your shoulders well back and a broad smile to make everyone present feel more at ease. The interviewer is probably quite nervous too. Shake hands if you can and remember to thank the interviewer for his or her time when you leave.

Make sure that you speak loudly and fully enough to do justice to your skills and strengths. The employer genuinely wishes to hear what you have to say so do not hold back from talking about yourself and your achievements. Imagine that I am a fly on the wall, urging you on to speak up, let your personality out and enjoy the experience. Good luck!

Step 4. Follow-up

It is wise to apply for more than one vacancy at a time, so you always have more interviews ahead of you. Be sure that each one is for a post that interests you though, otherwise you will not find the motivation to make an impressive application. This helps to keep a sense of perspective about the process and keeps you from feeling demoralised if you don't get a job. It is easy to become depressed about lack of success in job interviews. However, the most expert interviewees may be turned down just because, on the day, there happened to be somebody who seemed more suitable.

If you are rejected, it is worth contacting the employer to ask for some feedback on your performance in the interview. Most employers are keen to help as long as the request is phrased politely. I suggest something like:

'I have just attended an interview with you. Although I was not successful, I wondered if I could ask you for any feedback on my performance in the interview, as I am particularly interested in this type of work and your comments might help me in the future.'

Another antidote to feeling despondent about searching for work is to mix with other people in the same situation. A supportive group can keep you going when you feel at the end of your tether. At times you will need to fight the feeling that there is something wrong with you as a person. Sharing your experiences with other people will remind you that there are other excellent candidates who fail to get jobs. Maintaining some semblance of a work routine is also helpful in keeping up morale. Voluntary work, for example, provides contacts, experience, and a sense of purpose and self-worth. Some kind of study or training keeps you developing, gives you the chance to interact with others and can prove to be very rewarding.

If you keep getting invited to interviews then you know that your written applications are of a high standard. If you keep attending interviews, always doing your best and trying to improve, you will eventually get a job. Strongly resist feeling demoralised, depressed or unconfident. It was said earlier that interviews should be treated as learning experiences. Even if you are not successful at an interview, you can feel comfortable in the knowledge that you have done your best to create a good impression.

Learning from experience

Whenever you attend an interview make a note immediately afterwards of the questions you were asked and how you replied. Try and get the wording down exactly too. Evaluate what happened. Did any of the questions take you by surprise? If so, they need fuller preparation next time. Which of your answers seemed to go down well? Why was that? This exercise will prove very useful if you ever go for a similar vacancy, or apply to the same organisation in the future. It is also helpful to reflect on afterwards. Continuous improvement comes from looking back and learning in this way.

Other sources of help

The Connexions Service

In some areas of the country, the staff in your local connexions service can offer help and advice to adults. They will have reference books about employers and applying for jobs as well as understanding and skilled staff who can help you put your CV together if you get stuck. They may also help you plan and rehearse for an important interview, or refer you somewhere which can offer this type of assistance. Find the phone number in the local phone book and ring them to find out more.

Employment/Recruitment agencies

Agencies may help you prepare for a meeting with an employer for a particular type of job. They charge the employer if you are placed with a company.

Private career counsellors

You can get help from career counsellors who work privately and will make a charge for their service. This can be very expensive although they will help coach you for different interview situations.

Learn Direct

The Learn Direct number, 0800 100 900, is a Government funded telephone helpline available to everyone. Ring the freephone number and you will be given advice about local sources of help on career and learning issues. This could include where to contact the types of organisations mentioned above.

Internet resources

Using the Internet to help you with interviews

There are many Internet sites that give you assistance with interview techniques. Most are sites displaying job vacancies. They make their money from recruitment advertising by employers or by taking a commission from employers if they place you in a job. As part of the information they provide around searching for jobs these sites often include tips on interview skills and other career development issues.

Job seekers can access these pages free of charge, although if you want to use their specialised targeting process for locating the most relevant jobs to suit you, you may be required to go through a registration process.

The World Wide Web is a fast-changing scene and new sites appear as fast as others fall from view. Here are ten of the current best for UK job seekers.

1. www.prospects.ac.uk
Labelled as the UK's official graduate careers Web site, this site is provided by the Higher Education Careers Services Unit and the Association of Graduate Careers Advisory

Services. It is aimed at graduates and provides '...the essential guide to graduate careers and postgraduate study in the UK' according to the home page.

Accessible and functional, this is a useful resource for graduates and by gathering all the key points together can help to focus a graduate's job search or path to further study.

2. www.jobs.guardian.co.uk

'The UK's most popular newspaper Web site'. Provided by the *Guardian* newspaper group which is the national newspaper with the largest selection of jobs. Accessible and impressive, this site is easy to search for jobs by relevance to your needs. It has many new jobs every day, listed by broad sector and seniority.

This site is worth checking on a regular basis for national level jobs.

3. www.timesonline.co.uk

The Web site of *The Times* newspaper group. It contains Appointments – their jobs pages, particularly useful for senior vacancies, managerial, technical and secretarial jobs. The site also includes topical interview tips and career development articles.

4. www.ft.com

This is the recruitment site provided by the *Financial Times* newspaper. It includes job vacancies, particularly in the financial sector and some job search tips.

5. www.jobs.co.uk

Labelling itself 'The one-stop jobs supersite' this site searches all of the UK jobs boards for you to find vacancies that may suit you. It offers a list of sites that can help with interview techniques and assesses them for amount of information, ease of use etc.

This site includes CV and applications advice and links up direct to all the sites it finds for you.

6. www.doctorjob.com
Doctorjob is a careers publisher's Web site featuring a lot of careers information and graduate employment opportunities displayed in a quirky style with cartoons.

7. www.reed.co.uk
This site is owned by Reed employment, a leading employment agency. It includes voluntary opportunities and career tips including interview techniques.

8. www.bradleycvs.co.uk
A CV service company offering information about job search skills including interview techniques. This site also has many links to other specific recruitment sites.

9. www.monster.co.uk
A commercial recruitment Web site with extensive job search advice included.

10. www.jobpilot.co.uk
A recruitment Web site with some interview tips included.

Further reading from Kogan Page

Interview and career guidance

30 Minutes Before Your Job Interview, June Lines, 1997

The A–Z of Careers and Jobs, 10th edn, Irene Krechowiecka, 2002

Act Your Way Into a New Job, Deb Gottesman and Buzz Mauro, 1999

Changing Your Career, Sally Longson, 2000

Choosing Your Career, Simon Kent, 1997

Creating Your Career, Simon Kent, 1997

From CV to Shortlist, Tony Vickers, 1997

Graduate Job Hunting Guide, Mark Parkinson, 2001

Great Answers to Tough Interview Questions, 5th edn, Martin John Yate, 2001

How You Can Get That Job!, 3rd edn, Rebecca Corfield, 2002

The Job-Hunters Handbook, 2nd edn, David Greenwood, 1999

Job-Hunting Made Easy, 3rd edn, John Bramham and David Cox, 1995

Landing Your First Job, Andrea Shavick, 1999
Net That Job!, 2nd edn, Irene Krechowiecka, 2000
Odd Jobs, 2nd edn, Simon Kent, 2002
Offbeat Careers, 3rd edn, Vivien Donald, 1995
Online Job-Hunting: Great Answers to Tough Interview Questions, Martin John Yate and Terra Dourlain, 2001
Powerful Presentations, 3rd edn, Jöns Ehrenborg and John Mattock, 2001
Preparing Your Own CV, 3rd edn, Rebecca Corfield, 2003
Readymade CVs, 2nd edn, Lynn Williams, 2000
Readymade Job Search Letters, 2nd edn, Lynn Williams, 2000
Your Job Search Made Easy, 3rd edn, Mark Parkinson, 2002

Further advice on a variety of specific career paths can also be found in Kogan Page's *Careers in...* series and *Getting a Top Job in...* series. Please visit the Web site at the address below for more details.

Also from Kogan Page...

Career, Aptitude and Selection Tests, Jim Barrett, 1998
How to Master Personality Questionnaires, 2nd edn, Mark Parkinson, 2000
How to Master Psychometric Tests, 2nd edn, Mark Parkinson, 2000
How to Pass Advanced Aptitude Tests, Jim Barrett, 2002
How to Pass at an Assessment Centre, Harry Tolley and Bob Wood, 2001
How to Pass Computer Selection Tests, Sanjay Modha, 1994
How to Pass Graduate Psychometric Tests, 2nd edn, Mike Bryon, 2001
How to Pass Numeracy Tests, 2nd edn, Harry Tolley and Ken Thomas, 2000

How to Pass Professional-level Psychometric Tests, Sam Al-Jajjoka, 2001

How to Pass Selection Tests, 2nd edn, Mike Bryon and Sanjay Modha, 1998

How to Pass Technical Selection Tests, Mike Bryon and Sanjay Modha, 1993

How to Pass the Civil Service Qualifying Tests, Mike Bryon, 1995

How to Pass the Police Initial Recruitment Test, Harry Tolley, Ken Thomas and Catherine Tolley, 1997

How to Pass Verbal Reasoning Tests, Harry Tolley and Ken Thomas, 2000

Rate Yourself!, Marthe Sansregret and Dyane Adams, 1998

Test Your IQ, Ken Russell and Philip Carter, 2000

Test Your Own Aptitude, 2nd edn, Jim Barrett and Geoff Williams, 1990

Test Yourself!, Jim Barrett, 2000

The Times Book of IQ Tests – Book One, Ken Russell and Philip Carter, 2001

The Times Book of IQ Tests – Book Two, Ken Russell and Philip Carter, 2002

The above titles are available from all good bookshops. For further information, please contact the publisher at the following address:

Kogan Page Limited
120 Pentonville Road
London N1 9JN
Tel: 020 7278 0433
Fax: 020 7837 6348
www.kogan-page.co.uk

Index